Training
the
Versatile Retriever
TO HUNT UPLAND BIRDS

Look for Bill Tarrant's upcoming book,
Gun Dog Training Secrets of the Pros
Fall 1996

Books by Bill Tarrant

Best Way to Train Your Gun Dog

Hey Pup, Fetch It Up!

*Bill Tarrant's Gun Dog Book:
A Treasury of Happy Trails*

Tarrant Trains Gun Dogs

*Training the Hunting Retriever:
The New Approach*

Problem Gun Dogs

How to Hunt Birds with Gun Dogs

Pick of the Litter

*Training the Versatile Retriever
to Hunt Upland Birds*

Training
the
Versatile Retriever
TO HUNT UPLAND BIRDS

by
Bill Tarrant

Wilderness
Adventures
Press

Wilderness Adventures Press books are made to last for generations. They are printed on acid-free paper that will not turn yellow with age. The bindings are Smyth-sewn, allowing the books to open easily. Our binding boards are covered with 100% cloth. We commission today's top sporting artists to illustrate our books. We believe that our books are the finest sporting books published.

First Printing

Published by Wilderness Adventures Press
P.O. Box 627
Gallatin Gateway, MT 59730
800-925-3339

10 9 8 7 6 5 4 3 2 1

Printed in the United States of America

Library of Congress Catalog Card Number: 96-060858

ISBN 1-885106-28-9

for
Margaret Nichols, David Petzal, and Slaton White
who helped make it all go well

Table of Contents

Prologue

This book develops the concept of the versatile shooting retriever. It teaches you how to train and hunt a retriever for upland game.

Admittedly, the gene pool that makes a retriever fetch a bird is as old as dirt. What living thing does it better?

"Why then," you're probably asking, "would we now want a retriever to also do the work of a pointer or a flusher? Why have the retriever hunt up the bird for wing and shot, rather than just fetch the bird to hand? Why make retrievers something they're not? Why mess with a good thing?"

The answers are many and they're all vital to the future of American bird hunting.

For the world is unwittingly becoming anti-dog.

Real estate ads now advertise, "Oversized lots. All of 6,000 square feet." Where's a hunter going to put a kennel? Where's your gun dog, who lives in the house (where many of us want him), going to exercise ? And how can two or three dogs ever fit this postage-stamp lawn?

California just passed a law outlawing dogs in condos.

Some CC&Rs, those binding rules and regulations that go with some sub-divisions for homes, condos, townhouses, and mobile parks, state plainly, "No more than two dogs." Or, "No more than one dog and he must be less than 18 inches tall." That's right folks, these are facts. This is the way a great part of America is living: *and it's going to get worse.*

So you say, "Heck I won't put up with it, I'll just get me a piece of land out in the county." Priced an acre recently? I just moved from a county where you're hard put to find an acre for less than $100,000. Sure you can do better than that in Appalachia or the Ozarks...but if you're a highly-skilled journeyman, or a professional type, are jobs you want available there?

Plus, if you've got land you've got to tend it. Priced a tractor and bush-hog this year? Know what a power take-off and an augur cost?

If you don't drive a pickup, some cars are now the size of skate boards. Where's your two-dog team of pointer and retriever going to ride to the field?

Vet care has become astronomically expensive. Last year my wife and I paid $4,000 in an effort to make a dog's last months comfortable.

Where I use to pay $2.50 a hundred for bulk dog food I picked up at a granary in my flat-bed truck, today's nutritionally certified dog diets can cost a thousand bucks a year.

So when you add up the built-in expenses, and the limited space restrictions, you readily see why most of us can only afford one dog. And if we're going to hunt him on every type of game bird, he has to be totally versatile: he has to be able to do it all.

So enter the world of the versatile hunting retriever.

We got our first versatile dogs from Germany: they were the three German pointers, plus the Griffon, the Pudelpointer, and others. They were bred to point and fetch, work feather and fur, handle both field and water, and also run a blood trail. The guy who wanted a rabbit for lunch and a pheasant for dinner had the perfect dog in a German.

But the Germans were just a century ahead of us. And they had figured something out we still had to admit. That is: what gun dog species could exist today if its ancestors hadn't hunted and caught their food as well as fetched it to their young sometime in the past?

In other words, folks, every gun dog's got the seed in him to do it all. For I've done it all with setters, pointers, Brittanies, springers, and on and on. And more especially, the retrievers.

And why do I single out the retriever to be this Jack-of-all-trades? Because he's so good at it and it's a pleasure to be afield with him while he's doing it: especially on bobwhite.

Sure I've felt the power and mystery of an English pointer slammed to point, with his left leg braced to front, his right knee bent, his two rear legs far astraddle. His head jerked back and his nostrils dilated as he rakes the wind for scent of this stop to flush.

And I've laughed with joy at the spring of the spaniel, the joyous thrust of his head, the uncountable beat of his stubbed tail, as he snatches the trailing feathers from a squawking and wind-climbing pheasant.

But there's just something about a retriever–they're mellow, you know. And they're responsive. That's their hallmark. And they make you smile with their backward glance, their bull-dozing all cover aside as they admit no barriers, their surprising speed when they close for the fetch. And they bring it to you, laughing, and wait with such curiosity and self-pride as they watch you examine it, then stow it in your game bag. Then they leap and flip about in mid-air and they're off again with cocked ears and high tail. They're good to lie down with as you make a pillow of their rib-cage following a five mile walk. The two of you resting on the slope of a hill under a tall sycamore tree.

And you recall working the bobwhite and filling your limit only to be walking home to jump a pond dam and harvest two mallard drakes in their frantic explosion–for they knew they'd been had.

Versatile?

Ever have a retriever before your fireplace? Or feel the quiet assurance of the big fellow at the foot of your bed? Or caught the sound in the pickup's shell when the retriever's inner-clock knew sun-up was two hours away so he steadily thumped his tail to arouse you from your opening-day, fitful sleep?

Yes, if you want to go bird hunting, take a retriever. But that's not the way to say it. After you've finished this book you'll agree, "For the bird hunt of your life...let a retriever take you."

The Big Three Versatile Shooting Retrievers: (left to right) Chesapeake bay retriever, Labrador retriever, and golden retriever. Other retriever breeds exist, but these are the heavyweights.

Introduction to the Versatile Shooting Retriever

We lived in Kansas where bobwhite
went forty bushel to an acre and all
we had to hunt them with was retrievers.
It never occurred to us we were starting
the Hunting Retriever movement in America.

I'd rather be a black bear seeking stool in hackberry season than have to write about myself. But for the past 32 years I've worked to expand the retriever's role from a simple bird fetcher to a superb versatile shooting dog. And I've done what I could to expand the retriever's role from a waterfowl dog to an upland game specialist.

The result is retrievers that self-cast for upland game, work objectives, honor the bird's scent cone, hold the bird for the gunner either by sitting down, standing, or pointing, then fetch deadfall and lead the hunter to the covey's new location. All this has been accomplished with humane training techniques that leave all the dog in the dog. The result is three fold:

1) the retriever now uses all his God-given instincts,
2) for the first time the dog has the self initiative to take the man hunting, instead of the other way around,
3) and the retriever works the field because he wants to, not because he has to.

All this results from no-impact gun dog training based on FIDO. FIDO will be explained later but essentially it means the human partner and the gun dog develop together through shared communications, the deciphering of feed back, and the alteration of the message to gain desired performance. For a thorough explanation read *The Magic of Dogs*, by this author.

Since I've been involved in all this, there'll be a reference to myself from time to time; hackberry season or not.

JIM CULBERTSON

Having said that, let me introduce you to Jim Culbertson. This 59-year-old Fredonia, Kansas, native—long since moved to Wichita—is known today as a former Junior College All American guard, high school football coach, and retired athletic director.

Jim's built for stout—tough as old jerky, height and build of a tree stump, nearly bald, always sports a sly grin, and seldom leaves the bird field.

Jim was born into a hard-scrabble, big-hearted home short of necessities. So his father—a welder in a rural cement plant—taught him to hunt young to supply the table.

It was one of those shell-a-day propositions and Jim kept the family fed, plus later, extended his shooting by trading the widow women there abouts a bird for a shell. Jim was always thoughtful of those without.

It amuses me to vision those Fredonia merchants wondering why all those geriatric gals wanted a box of seven-and-a-halves. It would seem Jim came into this world clutching a Model-12 with which he became so adept he would shoot his first quail at 40 yards and the remainder at 80. Think not? Even today I'll cover all bets.

THE DOG PEDDLER

I met Jim 34 years ago on a June day in a pasture southeast of Wichita, Kansas. Jim had run an ad in the local paper announcing Lab pups for sale. I instantly took to the man's rogue and persimmon nature—he was a football coach who wanted to win, but also wanted to play.

6

Jim Culbertson, still looking fit, shows off tools of his trade: an intent Lab, a Model 12, and a handful of bobwhite.

At the same time Jim was pulling pranks on his students (no, I can't go into that, this is a family book), I remember a man was beating his son. So Jim took the boy away from the man–took him into his own home for a semester. And I heard Jim tell the father–they were out on the sidewalk–if he didn't like it he could fight right now and the man curled his fists but left the boy. Yet

7

the next day this very same boy might open his wall locker to have a mechanical snake leap into his face. The Coach would be peeking around a far corner.

I can't count the number of pro footballers, bankers, aircraft workers, lawyers, and also-rans who make an annual pilgrimage to Jim's house, to thank him for their school days. But those are not the reasons Jim leads off this book on hunting upland game with retrievers. No. The reason he's put up front is he's the man who started it all. It just evolved from necessity. Jim lived in Kansas, one of America's best bobwhite states, and his dogs were Labs. So, why not use them to hunt quail?

But note this: Labs are not the only great retriever. This book is written for all retrievers be they golden, Chessie, flat-coated, curly-coated, American or Irish water spaniel. This is their book, plus the guys (or gals) they take hunting.

THOSE NUTS WITH THEIR LABS

Soon after meeting Jim, I took to his Labs and his ways and we became (what you'd call) brothers. Plus, we became relentless upland-bird hunters all over mid-America. It mattered not what kind of bird, we'd put eight Labs down before us and vacuum a field clean. And the dogs could not out-hunt us. For in those days we could outwalk a Jeep–I well remember the day. While bird hunting, we tried to outrun two deer. Yes, we weren't bright but we were happy.

I also laugh at the remembrance of taking live birds fetched up by some zealot Lab and waiting till he left to release them to the wind. Do that while the dog was standing there and you'd have a mutiny.

Or the notion of hunting prairie chicken behind all those Labs up one flint-rocked, wind-swept knoll and down the other–like we were hunting for bobwhite with no cover–and going endless miles. The horizon was reached fifty times a day. That's how far we walked. And get a chicken? Maybe. But that wasn't the point. It was to be there with those dogs–they're clowns you know, and athletes, and buddies, and better hunters than we'll ever be. Want to learn to hunt upland birds: enroll under a retriever. And we think we train dogs to hunt. Ho!

Jim Culbertson (left) and author on unseasonably hot morning, hunting bobwhite in south-eastern Kansas.

All in all it wasn't long before Jim and I were known in those parts as those nutty quail hunters with the pack of Labs. Ridiculous, was the charge. Preposterous, was the consensus.

For you can imagine how dumbfounded a passing motorist would be to see a black wave of dogs swivel-hipping through a stand of pin oaks, or splashing down a creek, or circling an old den tree in bobwhite country.

9

GOING TO THE DOGS

The Labs became our lives. Training them, hunting them, field-trialing them, experimenting with them, loving them, vying with each other with the best each of us had—and folks, these weren't a bunch of pan-lickers. Our pack included bona fide field trial champions off the classic field trial circuit.

We'd be out there running blinds with those Labs in blizzards where you couldn't see the dog ten feet in front of you. Or we'd train in the dark of night. Don't think that won't put a nose on a dog!

And while hunting we'd wait until the other was straddling the fence to kick the birds up (you must always remember Jim's joshing ways). Knock each other sideways on the covey rise. Sneak blanks into each other's guns (would you believe I once ejected a pair of salt and pepper shakers Jim had secreted in the breech?).

Yes we were vigorous and untamed. But now it's like the Bible says: young men do and old men dream. Something like that. Look at it this way. Some young gal might fulfill your every visual fantasy—and that's what we'd have wanted in those days. But how about a gal 30 years older and 20 pounds heavier who goes to your neighbor and explains how you backed into his new car? Now you got something. For that's the way with old hunters. And old dogs.

And, as I think back, that's what we had with those Labs. Sure the English pointer would have stopped us breathless at his slam to point and anvil hold. Or the feisty English springer spaniel who laughed all the way across the field as he leaped five feet in the air to snatch the tail feathers from a launching pheasant. That would have left us breathless.

They're all to be treasured and loved.

WHAT'S A RETRIEVER?

But the Lab—*or any retriever*—they're the flag ship of the canine fleet. Dogged, determined, docile, doting. They will find any bird that's there. That's just their nose and their drive. Their nose—

I've had retrievers who would wind a bird on a Kansas knoll 400 yards away. It's no accident they are the preferred sniff dogs for bombs, dope, and various contraband.

Jim Culbertson and his youngest son, Wade, carry on the 30-year versatile shooting retriever tradition by directing Labs into hedgerow and then starting across field toward next stand of likely cover.

There's much to say for hunting. Here, Jim and Wade train nifty Lab during the '70s. Lifetime bonds develop between father and son, as well as between human partner and retriever.

And retrievers do their work calmly, like some old boy coming to work in a pair of overalls toting a lunch bucket. Plus they can do it like a crashing football halfback, never wincing as the dog surges through a stand of multi-flora rose and comes out with bird in mouth and a slash of blood across his nose. And yes, they can do it feverishly, like Jim's FC and AFC Keg of Black Powder who was so small she'd leap up at the casting line like a praying mantis to mark the field trial birds down.

Jim and Wade could not let a bird season pass without hunting together.

But mostly, retrievers are a loaf of bread and pound of baloney, sitting in the shade of a crab apple tree next to some cross-roads store. Moaning there beside you, licking their callused feet, looking up with those agate-colored eyes, smiling, telling you they love you—and for you to quit screwing around and let's get going.

THINKING BACK

I wonder now how Jim and I could have walked that far, shot that fast, ate that much Spam, and endured those slam-jolt badger holes and iced-up dawns? Stoved up the way I am now, I could no more scrape the diarrhea out of those dog crates, kneel in the field to sew up the chest of some dog that slammed into a half-buried piece of galvanized steel, eat that Kansas dust in a pheasant patch, or go leg-shaking down some row crop to rid a Devil's claw cinching my ankle.

Or could I?

ULTIMATE TRAINING

The result of everything that happened to Jim and me formed the natural outcome of the New Hunting Retriever movement. We had unlimited training facilities and personnel to try everything novel, plus we were hunting the bird-basket of America: Kansas. And we had bright dogs—which you will learn is vital for a shooting retriever. If it was a game bird, those retrievers brought it to bag.

In other words, we found out exactly what a retriever could do.

In training we could experiment with anything since Jim had—what was it—a 40-man football team? And they'd do anything to please the Coach. Did you ever see 20 bird boys in the field? Ten of them planting blinds? Have you ever had 10 marks down? Have you ever had 20 boys standing behind the line—with three cackling cock pheasants shot immediately before the dog—and should the dog break, the 20 of them would rush forward, mock-maul the dog, and scream, and seize him up and run with him high over their heads—and never, never, never would that dog ever break again.

Have you ever drawn from 40 boys to have them climbing every flour mill in the county trapping pigeons for training? Or looking under every bridge, checking every feed lot?

We had birds to train with and there's nothing you can't teach a dog—if you've got a bird.

And when we went hunting, we had quail populations second only to Texas – plus prairie chicken, pheasant, and dove. I'd say Jim and I cultivated (during each summer) the friendship of every Kansas farmer and access to his property come hunting season. My specialty was handing out alarm clocks to farm wives. Don't know why that worked, but it did. We literally had permission to hunt a zillion upland game-bird acres.

To say our Labs were laser-beamed, full-bored-nose, muscle-clumped, frenzy-driven, remote-controlled, yet self-minded bird hunters would be to say the obvious if you ever saw them in the field. And should that be your interest–then visit Jim in Wichita today, still running a pack of Labs after anything that can get off the ground.

PLAYING FAVORITES

Gun dogs and game birds have been my life, and retrievers have been my passion. As I travel about the country putting the ink on gun dogs and the men and women they take hunting, I'm constantly asked, "What is your favorite dog?" And I advisedly answer, "Whatever you're runnin'." For I must be impartial: since I want to help every man and woman who trains and hunts any conceivable gun dog breed alive, after any known legal-season bird that flies.

BUY THAT DOG A DRINK

But take the immortal retriever trainer, D. L. Walters, who still trains dogs and occasionally writes a training book. D. L. loved all his Labs but it was FC & AFC Sam Frizel of Glenspey he brought into his motel room at night to share a scotch and soda. D. L. didn't do that with the other Labs in his string. Sam was special.

So it is that I favored and did more with retrievers–and among them the Labs–than with all other working dogs. Though there were times in my kennels I had 29 tenants of my own, including English setters, Brittanies, border collies, Labs, English springer- and Welsh springer-spaniels, English pointers, Irish setters, Australian cattle dogs, a pair of coyotes, and in the house a passel of what-not dogs.

I loved and trained them all and hunted those who were up to it. For I kept a dog till he died. And kept him good–and hunted him if he wanted to go.

But most of you know the story. Arthritis drove me to the desert for climate and treatment and I had to close up the kennels. But not my heart, nor my mind. Dogs are still my love and my life. My work and my devotion. And Labs are the dogs that made me whatever I've become. And taught me whatever I know.

GOING AFIELD

So now we're interested in hunting upland game with retrievers. And my concern in starting this thing off isn't what I should put in it, but what must I leave out. For there's no way the world of upland game and retrievers can be encased in one book. So I promise. I'll make sure the important stuff's included.

WE'VE MET BEFORE

For you see I know you, and I won't let you down. I see each of you in my mind's eye, as I've seen you—and met and talked to you—so many thousand times. Both of us out hunting a soy bean field, or in the kafir corn, or walking the endless expanse of CRP (or as we called it in the old days: "land banks").

I've met you coming through a crackling field of milo after pheasant, kicking about in the sand plum thicket for bobwhite, checking this year's crop of nut grass for Mearns quail, walking beside the irrigation ditches for their California cousins. Yes, we've both been there, hunting the desert sky-islands for scaled quailed, casting our retrievers into wolf willows for huns and sharptail.

Hearing each other call out, "I got him," as we shot a blue grouse in a mountain meadow 10,000 feet up, or hurried to an abandoned apple orchard—at a much lower elevation—to find their ruffed relatives.

And I've been there with you when the mourning dove jetted over the corn fields of Dixie, and I've seen you walk the endless expanse of the Kansas flint hills seeking the solitary prairie chicken.

You'll remember I was the guy with the four Labs, and we talked a while behind the shelter of a bluff, and took a long drink of water, and felt the wind chill our sweat, as we rested after hunting all morning in that straight-up-and-down chukar country.

Maybe you remember me, too? But it doesn't really matter. What matters is this hunt we're going to make now. And the way we're going to train to make the best of all gun dogs. Just you and your retrievers and me. So let's cast our dogs and get started.

If you're like me, there's nothing else on earth you'd rather do.

THE YEARS PASS

But just a moment. What happened to Jim? He went on to retire and now works at Boeing. And me? I went with *Field & Stream.*

Some 26 years later I wrote a book, *Hey Pup, Fetch It Up!* that—with no intention on my part—laid the groundwork for the hunting retriever movement in America. Because those who read this book for the first time realized the classic field trial circuit was detrimental to the breeding, training, and handling of any bona fide hunting retriever.

Hey Pup! made graphic the fact that judges conducted nonhunting tests so *contrary to a dog's nature* the tests demanded retrievers trip over their God-given instincts in order to pass them. And when the dogs wouldn't or couldn't do it, *they were too often brutalized into compliance.* I demanded an end to this insanity since the classic field trial circuit was supposed to be duplicating a day's hunt afield—instead of something a fiend would think up for a Dachau for dogs.

The classic retriever field trial tests evolved and continued with a nonhunter intent (and still do). Why, the handler can't even handle a gun! You call that hunting? What's the guy supposed to do, throw rocks at the birds? And except for a walk-up (where the handler and gunner walk the field to encounter a planted or thrown bird) the handler never leaves the casting line, and there is nothing done in a field trial to approximate actual hunting (except for fetching pheasants and ducks). *In other words, the dog is never cast to find the bird before it's shot. He is maintained as a retrieving retriever, never a shooting retriever.*

Anyway, retrievers have for years been tested as nonhunters. The philosophy in training for these trials was to fetch-the-poultry-at-all-cost. One pro trainer explained to me, "On a water blind that dog's got to be more scared of me than what's out there." And you call that training a hunting retriever?

Scared of me! What the hell's that got to do with anything? That dog should be bonded to his human partner with love—where the look of disappointment in your face hurts more than if another man hit the dog with a two-by-four.

Now *hurt* doesn't just mean physical pain. A trainer's attitude can be negatively overpowering. There is terror of countenance. I've seen dogs fold at a rough man's voice or cower from an

17

intimidating man's approach. The man may never have been physically brutal with the dog, but psychologically he has given the dog a bowling-ball-sized ulcer.

Anyway, in years of training and calling on dog trainers all over the world, I learned shooting a dog with bird shot, beating him with a BB-loaded whip, shocking him with a high voltage, low amperage electric collar, is simple, out-and-out stupidity and brutality. I also learned a love-run dog can outhunt a whip-run dog any day of the week on any bird field.

OMAR DRISKILL

While all this was going on, a grizzled duck guide and scrape-it-out-of-the-dirt, hunting-retriever trainer down in Simsboro, Louisiana, named Omar Driskill, had his old Lab named Wags pass away and Omar wrapped Wags in his grimy hunting coat and buried him beneath his bedroom window. Standing there crying with a face as ragged as a Nevada mountain crest, Omar realized there was no way this dog could be remembered, no way he could be honored for what he was.

All the world could not bestow enough praise on this retriever, who had fetched 499 out of 500 ducks for Omar's commercial clients every legal season; whose duck camp was 10 miles from the nearest landfall; who had fetched ducks and geese shot in every kind of weather and terrain from sunken blinds in the delta, the rice pits of the plains, and the flooded timber of the swamps–a slim-built Labrador retriever who was a bona fide, journeyman Field Trial Champion in the bird field–not in the game-people-play field. This dog died with no more honor than a mud-crusted hunting coat and a hand-dug grave beneath his human partner's bedroom window.

Here was the real Hunting Retriever Champion above the field trial champion–and there was no way to give Wags his due.

So standing there, looking at that mound of dirt, Omar with his grimed-and-gnarled hands, the dirt caked under his fingernails, the dried mud stuck to his knees, the frayed cuffs and tattered shirt, the wind biting his cheeks, Omar VOWED this would never happen again.

Hunting retrievers would be awarded for the excellence of their work.

Omar Driskill teaches a Chessie to mark off gun: this trainer's specialty. Remember, Omar trains duck dogs, and a dog that marks off the gun has a head-start in knowing where birds are going down.

BOB RATHE

And further south, in Covington, Louisiana, a scrubbed-bright, thirtyish, business executive with a partial-walrus mustache that seemed odd with a buttoned-down collar and proper Ivy League neck tie, this guy named Bob Rathe, had grown weary and disillusioned with the classic field trial circuit and envisioned a test format where hunting retrievers could be developed and tested.

You know the type. Bob was a young shaker and doer. A future internet sophisticate.

I like to remember Bob as the guy who walked into a New Orleans bank for parking change. The clerk told him he had to have an account. Bob opened one. Got his parking change and closed the account.

Bob had put on the classic field trials, found the birds, got the bird boys, ordered the judge's gifts, made sure there was a hostess

19

committee, and got the hot dog cart through the mud to the center of the field trial grounds.

And when years and years of this were finished, Bob Rathe realized he was upholding a sport that had nothing to do with his primary interest–and that was to put his boys and his Labs in the Jeep and go bird hunting.

FIELD & STREAM

Now while Omar and Bob were moving toward the same point of view, a series of gun dog columns in *Field & Stream* kept hammering away to describe and promote hunting retrievers in America.

Finally, in the April 1983 issue of *Field & Stream*," a column appeared titled, "The Mechanical Dog." Omar Driskill read that article and just like that, stood, stuffed some clothes in a battered duffel, and launched a no-money, personally-fatigueless, national crusade. He left his dog-training business, his wife and kids, and struck out–going anywhere anyone would listen, demanding a new test format for retrievers be created–a test format created by hunters for hunters, where dogs were tested on typical things that happened everyday in the hunting field; and no dog would compete against another.

Instead, they would run against par, thus so much of the rancor would be removed from dog tests. You know, handlers always griping about how their dog got robbed. It was a singular hardship for Omar. His income vanished, his health was strained, his home life estranged. But he kept crusading.

Then the first national interests crested, and here and there bona fide hunters began to pay Omar and the magazine articles heed, and finally the dam broke and all over the nation. These good ol' boys surged forward to create the hunting retriever clubs of America.

UNITED KENNEL CLUB

Finally, Fred Miller invited the three retriever men mentioned above to his United Kennel Club (UKC) headquarters in Kalamazoo, Michigan, where, along with his sons and Andy Johnson, magazine editor for UKC, the Hunting Retriever Club was founded in 1983.

It proved fate does have its own plodding but inevitable way, when 13 years after *Hey Pup* was published, a line drawing on page 314 of the book that started it all, was selected as the trademark of the new Hunting Retriever club.

GETTING IT GOING

The first hunting retriever test conducted in America where championship points were awarded, was held in Ruston, Louisiana, in April 1984, where Omar Driskill, Bob Rathe, and this writer (along with others, since there were several stakes) judged the first hunting retrievers where points were awarded on actual hunting tests

On the Club's 10th anniversary–and now with branch clubs all over America–the old-timers got together in Ruston, Louisiana, for a joyful April 1994 reunion and a granddaddy hunting retriever test.

So now you see how the hunting retriever movement came about due to the following motives that provided the fuel:

1. This writer was the idea man who became known as the Godfather of the Hunting Retriever Movement. He didn't want these dogs hurt.

2. Omar was the evangelist. He took the word to the most remote haunts of this nation. Omar wanted a way to reward retrievers who had given their lives in service to the gun. He was the first HRC president.

3. And Bob Rathe was the organization man. He wanted a format to test retrievers as hunters, so his dogs would be ready to take him and his sons bird hunting. He set the standards with his local retriever club holding test hunts and sponsoring seminars. He quit quickly since he saw the HRC movement was doomed by the nonhunter leadership and the field trial imitators long before it became evident to Omar and this writer. We were just hoping too much.

Anyway, in the beginning, these three diverse interests ultimately accomplished the one common goal: The Hunting Retriever.

TEN YEARS LATER

At that 10th anniversary meeting there was a lot of hoopla about the above mentioned being responsible for the hunting retriever movement in America and the Hunting Retriever club. But I want all of you to remember this: *Field & Stream,* with its 14,500,000 readers, is where the campaign was conducted. *Field & Stream* is the wagon on which the hunting retriever rode into reality.

WHERE CREDIT'S DUE

And one final thing. At that initial meeting of the board, we created the first board of directors: *Jim Culbertson's name led the list.*

THEN FINALLY

While all the above was going on, a group of eastern retriever enthusiasts formed the North American Hunting Retriever Association (NAHRA) to accomplish the same aims. The spearhead of this eastern movement once asked this author why there had to be two retriever movements, saying, "They'll only be half as much." I answered him, saying, "No…they'll be twice as much," and so they proved to be.

But where I hoped two windows would produce twice the light, it hasn't worked out that well as we shall see later in this book. The hunting retriever is alive and capable in the bird field, filling the game bag and his human partner's pride, as well. But at test hunts the judges have dipped back into all I hoped to destroy.

Once again they are conducting nonhunting tests that too often require the retriever trip over his God given instincts to pass. Failing in that, these retrievers can then be beat or beat-down by a pro or amateur who just has no fertilizer in his plot (I mean folks, this guy's brain is sterile).

Unfortunately, there are some who now judge at test hunts who have little notion of what a hunting retriever should be. For they've never actually taken a retriever bird hunting. They've probably taken one bird retrieving: but not bird hunting.

So we're back in that inhumane quagmire I fought to eliminate these past twenty years. The dead hand of the old classic retriever field circuit is once again choking the life out of the new hunting retriever. But that doesn't mean the hunting retriever clubs of America have to self destruct. They can be saved. The seeds for rediscovery and rededication are planted in this book.

AMERICAN KENNEL CLUB

Now, lets back up. With all the interest in the hunting retriever ten years ago, a gun dog man asked an American Kennel Club official what AKC thought about all these efforts. The man replied, "If it were needed, we would have it."

Years later AKC must have decided, "...it were needed," for they instituted their own hunting retriever format and invited many of us back east for a demonstration. Through three days it amused me to note AKC acted as if no one had ever thought of the hunting retriever before. No mention was ever made of the pioneers, and the established national clubs, and all the Hunting Retriever Champions who had been crowned, and everything else that established the hunting retriever movement as reality.

At this date all three clubs (HRC, NAHRA, and AKC) are still testing the hunting retriever.

HUMANE SEMINAR AND VSR WORKSHOP

But no organization is testing the versatile shooting retriever. Now you and I aren't really interested in some test format for dogs. What we want is a sure'nuf shooting dog to take us upland bird hunting. Right? So what we're going to do in this book is show you how to train your retriever to hunt, then three old friends I've trained with for years, and a new convert to my training teachings, are going to accept an invitation to attend the first humane training seminar and versatile shooting retriever workshop ever conducted.

BOB BURLINGAME'S FLYING B RANCH

All this takes place at Bob Burlingame's Flying B Ranch, in Kamiah, Idaho. We are mighty indebted to Bob for permitting us total use of his world-class hunting and fishing lodge. Let me tell you how this came about.

For the ten years I've known Mike Gould, gun dog trainer extraordinaire, he's moved his diggin's up and down the west slope of the Colorado river. I'd visit Mike nearly every summer and we'd train and talk and fish and hit the high country and just live God's life.

On hand with Mike would usually be a sporting good store manager named Butch Goodwin, who is an accomplished Chesapeake bay retriever trainer, and Gary Ruppel, who is now pioneering in the training of pointing Labs.

Then suddenly everyone was cast to the wind. Mike threw in with Bob Burlingame to manage his Idaho holdings. Butch turned Chessie pro and moved to New Plymouth, Idaho. And Gary opened up a successful gun dog training kennel at Parker, Colorado.

So I got to thinking how great it would be if we could all get together again. We're like feathers you know, and flock well. So I asked Mike if he'd see what Bob Burlingame thought about inviting all of us up. Bob sprung for it. What a treat. So we all met.

I included in the group a recent acquaintance of mine, the mild and soft mannered Jim Charlton of Portland, Oregon, who has the odd reality of being a Golden retriever specialist.

Going afield with this lot is just a fun way of closing out the book, five old retriever pros with their dogs, hunting upland birds in that high country of northern Idaho.

AVOID THE MESS

So let's climb in this old flap-fendered pickup of mine and get going. But wait—are there any shells in that gun? Doc Moore, an old hunting buddy of mine in Hoisington, Kansas, had a hole blown in the floorboard of his International Scout. Tom Ness, the spaniel trainer in Bismark, North Dakota, was shot in his back while driving a party of hunters to bag sharptail.

So keep those damned shells in your pocket 'til we get there. Or I'll tell my dogs to dump in your hat while we're eating lunch. What? Yes, they've been trained to do that.

What? Take my word for it: you really don't want to find out.

Later in this book I'll tell you bobwhite avoid heavy cover like this, but after shooting this photo, Jim Culbertson's forward-coursing Lab knocked up a sizable covey in this tangle.

Here's Jim Culbertson with part of his 1960s pack. There's nothing that can equal the fun and the thrill, or the productivity and the unequaled success, of bird hunting with a pack of retrievers.

26

The New Do-It-All Retriever

*You wouldn't buy a Jeep Wrangler if the
salesman told you it could only be driven
in low-low. So why would you own a
retriever that could only fetch dead birds?*

There are thousands of guys and gals I want to help: they've
bought a gun and now they want to get a dog to go upland
bird hunting. Well, it's important to me these hopefuls get a leg
up: **So we'll show them through this book why they should
choose a versatile shooting retriever!**

A versatile shooting retriever?

Yep, that's a retriever who can barely wait for you to get out of
the pickup, who dumps and dallies no longer than it takes you to
don your gear and get your gun, then self-casts. That's right, he self-
casts, for he (or she) knows what they're doing. Why wait for you?

Heading for points of opportunity (places he/she knows the
birds will be) the versatile shooting retriever decodes the wind,
humidity, pollen, nature of the terrain, cover, species of bird he's
learned uses this habitat, and whatever else the genius of a bona
fide gun dog takes into account. I even suppose a shooting
retriever knows the relative humidity. For here's the clincher:
these dogs were making a living in the field long before they ever
threw in with man. Man says, "I trained him to hunt." Ha!

All man ever trained a dog to do was obey: the hunt was
already in the dog. And all that obeying has been a yoke about
the dog's neck, a curse driven through his soul.

When the versatile shooting retriever enters the covey's scent
cone he tells you what he's found–in this book we'll teach you

what he's saying and how he's saying it so you can **read*** your dog. Then depending on what you've trained this gun dog to do, the versatile shooting retriever whoas (either sitting or standing), points, or flushes.

This do-it-all retriever then recasts to fetch deadfall, plus, since he's watched the covey relocate, he waits until you're ready, then takes you for a second flush.

And that's the versatile shooting retriever: the dog who takes you hunting, not the other way around. The maximum bird-producing dog you'll ever put before a gun. And at no time do I know of any retriever (except a handful we'll talk about later) who was ever given his head, his heart, his legs, or his nose like I describe here. Always the retriever has been held back, restricted, denied. Tell me, when has a retriever ever been given the opportunity to do anything on his own? Oh yes, there is this exception: some were let loose in pheasant fields to barge in and knock those snake-tails to the wind. But that was it!

DOMINATION

Man has always dominated the retriever. Always demanded the man take the dog hunting, instead of the other way around. Heel, Sit, Stay, Back, Stop, Over, Back, Come in, Stop, Over, NO DAMN IT, Back, remember? Always letting the dog know the man possesses more knowledge and instinct about the bird and the bird field than the dog will ever know.

But no more.

For today's the dawn of emancipation for both you and the retriever. A day both of you had to wait a hundred years to ever come about. Thank God for both dog and man it happened now.

I said **"read" up there. Read your dog. Know what I mean? It's so simple. I was hunting chukar with a Lab named Rowdy today. Ol' Rowdy couldn't get the sleep out of his eyes. He was indefinite, puttering, when suddenly everything in Rowdy woke up. He turned to the left, took a draw on the wind, and ran head-up toward a scattering of yucca. Rowdy just remembered he was chukar hunting, and he recalled from last year that's where he always found them. And that's reading.*

28

THE RETRIEVER'S TRADITIONAL ROLE

This most versatile of all gun dogs started his life's work on English estates fetching deadfall and was called a non-slip retriever. Which meant the dog didn't cast until the leash was released from his neck and man directed him to and fro.

It was the age of the gentry and robber barons. The last vestige of the feudal era where the Lord of the manor called the shots and had scores of servants to do his bidding. Thus it was a caste system: and that's the way the dogs were restricted. The pointer found the bird, the retriever fetched the bird. To ask an Englishman for the retriever to do anything more, you'd be told in that tiny isle's inimitable suck-tooth way, "It just isn't done."

And I do repeat: what was considered "hunting the retriever" was for the gentry to assemble all their retainers (or in my day the available village men), give each of them a tall staff with a great flag, then intersperse among them some retrievers, and have them beat toward the butts with the men yelling like banshees. Oh yes I've done it. And the grouse do come thundering. But…think again…is this what I mean by a versatile shooting retriever? No!

And so it was that this "caste" system prevailed even to America in the 20th century, when the Mr. Moneyfellers of Long Island imported the first retrievers and "stole" their keepers to accompany them.

But nothing was changed. The pointers still found the birds and the retrievers remained *canine morticians*: doing nothing more than gathering up dead birds after the hunt was over.

And ain't it mind blowing to realize the retriever could have equaled, or maybe outhunted, the pointer all that time? For Jim Culbertson and I have seen that in the bird field. In later years we'd take along a Brit out of my kennel, or an English pointer or setter, or whatever. And the retrievers would have the bird dogs humping to contribute their share to the game bag. But the dead hand of the past has always held man (and dog) down. Yes, folks, even with this book being bought and read, some of this will last forevermore.

Now don't think you won't find protests to what I'm saying. There are those who'll tell you their retrievers do it all in the field. They'll say, "Why I've always hunted my field trial retrievers...what the hell you talking about?"

Well, running a retriever in a wild-bird field instead of a test format ain't necessarily hunting. Not if the dog is limited to scouring the patch (carrying his stretcher, if you will) looking for the dead and wounded...and doing only as the handler commands. You might say the retriever has only been used for carrion: never given the opportunity to find a live bird.

Seldom have these people who say they've hunted their retrievers ever sent the dogs to scent live game in the first place, trained them to hold it until the gunner was ready, then produce the bird for wing and shot, and finally fetch up what was hit and take the hunter to the next covey. Seldom? Maybe once? Never!

But that's exactly what you and I—along with Pup—are going to do.

NOT FIT FOR A DOG

Now that I've repeated that word-triplet VERSATILE SHOOTING RETRIEVER enough times, it should be indelible in your mind. So let's shorten it to save book paper and give us an easier handle to carry the concept around. From now on, this do-it-all dog will be known as the VSR. Okay?

THE HUNTING RETRIEVER MOVEMENT

Now I've told you I thought I'd witnessed a breakthrough in 1983 with the inauguration of the hunting retriever clubs, and I went away whistling a tune called, "High Hope."

But there's another song I should have known would be the second verse: "Don't know why there's no sun up in the sky: stormy weather."

For in ten years I saw the hunting retriever movement revert right back to the insane and inimical testing format I'd fought to eliminate. And the essential reason? The new hunting retriever contestants felt second class to the classic field trial people and decided to emulate them. They didn't want hunting dogs, they wanted mechanical dogs. Dogs forced to perform meaningless tests that might be duplicated in a day's hunt afield once in every ten years.

THEIR INTEREST IS NOT OUR STANDARD

So here's the book to scuttle every thing presently being done with our retrievers. Here's the book to acclaim the shooting retriever, instead of the retrieving retriever. Here's the book to put the shooting retriever in charge in the field and have the man come along. To let the dog dig deep to find his old instincts that we've beat out of him. To see his genius arise again in puzzling out quarry, to see him think things out on his own instead of being ordered to do this and do that. And the joy for the dog! Ha. Well just figure: today the retrievers get their own Emancipation Proclamation.

Talk about delighted. You've never seen a happy dog until you've seen a bunch of shooting retrievers out hunting bobwhite.

So welcome to this break-out day of the most magnificent animal God ever put on earth. Welcome to this new day of the VSR.

A day where if you ain't got one, you're leaving a bird in every other bush. And leaving a continuous smile, as well, back in your pickup.

SPIRIT! The author's Lab pack rapidly clears a knoll in quest of bobwhite. Tails spew water since they just stopped at a farm pond to drink.

From the Dog's Point of View

It came to pass dogs ruled the world.
This man asked a retriever if he could
go hunting with him, and the retriever
said, "Yes, if you'll ride a unicycle, throw
only rocks, and never aim with your eyes."
And the man said, "That's impossible."
And the retriever said, "No, that's a pay-back."

The ideal for training a dog is stroking, not striking. Enticing, not intimidating. Smiling, not frowning. Thinking, not threatening. In other words, the trainer's attitude is more important than the devices he uses to train. Both good devices, and bad devices. Some that help the dog self-train, that facilitate his own coming out, and others that force the dog through pain to perform.

For know these two things. You can take the spirit out of a dog but you can't put it back in. And, if a dog makes you mad he's defeated you. So in all things with a gun dog, put your best foot forward, not the toe of your boot.

And know this. A dog knows what you think of him. If he's loved he'll repay you a thousand fold. If he's merely endured, he'll sulk and become depressed and never have a laughing moment.

I once knew a horrible man who'd go down into Arkansas and buy a bird dog for a few bucks, hunt him all season, then leave him along side the road when the season was over. That man never had a good dog. That man's dogs all resented him, performed lethargically, showed disgust in their eyes.

But I know another man who had the ability to go to the dog pound and pick out a mongrel gun dog and put the bluebloods to shame by the time he got the dog trained and motivated—and kept! So watch your attitude. Pup will.

A WORD ABOUT FIELD TRIALS AND TEST HUNTS

My advice is so different from old-time training books that told us to assemble an arsenal of give-in devices, tell the dog what we wanted him to do and if he didn't do it, then fire our entire arsenal onto his hide and into his psyche.

A DIFFERENT KIND OF BOOK

This ain't that kind of book. This book shows you how to train a VSR using conventional methods only with humane techniques, then we'll get into an exciting new form of gun dog training right from the womb by primarily using wide country and wild birds. Then you choose which way you want to go (or have to go if you can't get to land or birds). Both systems work. Only the second system works better.

And know this. I've written several books that will train a classic field trial retriever, plus hunting retrievers for test hunts, and nonslip retrievers for the bird field. Refer to them if that's the retriever you want. However, in this book we learn how to train and hunt a VSR for upland game: where the dog finds the bird, not just fetches it.

NOT DONE BEFORE

Until now, versatile shooting retrievers have not generally been trained, bred, whelped, adopted, nor used in the bird field, nor recognized by the retriever experts, nor the general hunting public. Incredible isn't it?

HUNTING UPLAND GAME

I just received the Hunting Retriever Club's rules and guidelines for hunting retriever tests effective this year. They now incorporate upland hunt tests in their rule book. But alas, for the most part, they fall back into the same nonshooting strait jacket for the dog.

First, they don't even separate the upland hunt tests in the table of contents. Then they attach the actual upland hunt test guidelines to the bottom of the explanation of what a finished hunting retriever test may include.

But get this. For the most part, when the HRC uses the term hunting retriever, it is meant the retriever hunts for dead game, not for live game for the hunter to shoot. What a vast difference.

Also, it is stated the upland test, "...will consist of a simulated walk-up hunt with a subsequent quartering or tracking test."

Now that don't get it.

A walk-up too often constitutes a dog at heel. Along the path man and dog encounter either a planted or thrown, live or dead bird. At no time is the retriever released to actually go out on his own and hunt up live game.

And as for the quartering or tracking? This has no application to a versatile shooting retriever unless he's beating a CRP field or a venue of planted row crops. Know why? Well a VSR's beat depends upon the terrain and cover.

How, I ask you, is a VSR going to quarter a dense stand of pin oaks for bobwhite, or a brush tangle within a pinched creek bank for woodcock? With such natural obstacles the VSR is going to snake his way through.

And as for trailing spoor—I know of few dogs of any breed who won't follow out a blood trail. And I've never had a retriever who wouldn't do it—without any training! But then I've often found a retriever to be superior to all other gun dogs in nose, intelligence, aptitude, bidability, and verve.

AN ADVANCED UPLAND GAME TEST

Then in the section listing Guidelines for Judging Finished Hunting Retrievers, the book says this:

"Quartering: The dog hunts in a radius ideally from 10 to 30 yards to the side and in front of the Handler. The live bird is released (or thrown) in full view of the dog." Let me interrupt. This is just a long distance walk-up. The dog is walking along (this time in front of the man) and a bird boy throws a bird from the bush: the dog does not scent out and uproot any bird. The bird appears from nowhere: it is a fool bird to leap before being detected. Heh, what?

Well, that isn't a retriever being sent to locate a game bird. Or a retriever to work the cover and terrain, to know what he seeks, to go to likely objectives, to enter the bird's scent cone, and to wait for the man to be in position to shoot. Okay, to continue.

"The distance from the bird to the dogs," says the manual, "should be within scent distance when the bird is released. The dog is required to be steady to wing and shot. The dog should immediately return to the previous hunting range upon being called and/or whistle commanded by the Handler. The Handler will shoot the gun (popper), and the gunners may kill the bird. If the dog does not immediately return to the hunting area, the test is failed."

Now all this evades me. Where in the hell did the dog go—why does he have to return from where? But it makes no difference. The HRC is not going to test a retriever out hunting upland game. They're going to play the same old classic field trial game: limiting the retriever to be a canine mortician. And get this, too. Why can't the hunter shoot? A popper is a blank shell. Who do you bring along with you to do your shooting? Don't think dogs don't know all this stuff is phony. They're bright. They know.

The manual then says, "The dog should be eager, hunt all available cover diligently and be under control." But the manual never says he should use his nose. The manual never says he should actually hunt. And why doesn't the manual go into detail about wind, cover, terrain, humidity, and light?

Then it is announced, "The intent of the Quartering test is not to demonstrate running a pattern, but to demonstrate natural tendency to hunt and be under control." Well, that's fine and that's needed. But when is the test hunt retriever hunting with his nose? When is he winding and uprooting the bird? He ain't. So how could they say he was hunting? And as for control—let the dog be under his own control. Let him have his own head. Damn this domination.

THAT MEANS THERE'S NO ORGANIZED CLUB TO HELP US

So it leaves it entirely up to us to develop the retriever we all must have and we all want: the VSR. The restrictive hand of the past still hobbles the shooting retriever. The premise remains: dominance. Man must dominate the dog's performance, his life, and his hunt. Never is the retriever permitted to do anything on his own. Man must do all the thinking, and the dog do all his bidding.

When my friends, it must be the other way around.

SO WE'VE ALL BEEN DUMB?

Now, no one's ignorant because they haven't realized what a retriever can do. Hell, no one showed anybody what a retriever could do. Everyone was tradition- and stimulus-bound. Only a handful of people knew what the retriever was capable of doing–and we weren't hanging around field trials, we were out hunting. Don't think Jim Culbertson and I ever entered our retrievers in a field trial during hunting season.

And this is important. It was twenty years later before I met another man hunting his Labs. And that was Mike Gould. Twenty years to find one man.

So it's only now you'll learn about every retriever's unlimited versatility and his excellence above all other gun dogs in harvesting game. By the time you read the last page of this book the retriever will have been elevated in its ability to handle the field from a flatbed wagon pulled by a team of oxen to a Land Rover.

And a pleasure to be with! I've never seen anything as joyous as a VSR out hunting.

AND TO DO ALL THIS

First, we won't commit any of the old errors any more. For example, never again will there be any harshness in retriever training. *We will train with intimacy, not intimidation.* Why? Well liken this to some gal (or for you gals, some guy) who seeks a lover. What would be the guaranteed way to go about it? How about beating her, scolding her, denying her, humiliating her, and just generally being a bullish ass?

Or do you think this would work? Start pampering her, telling her what a great gal she is, taking her with you wherever you go, adoring her, caring for her, and swearing before her you'll never leave her so long as you both shall live, and then gently and intimately showing her just what you want her to do. And give her every opportunity to do it!

Wonder which guy (or gal) will get the lovin'?

THE BONDED VSR

On the basis of the only answer there can be to the question asked, *we will henceforth bond with our dog.* And the result? We'll create a VSR, who out of desire to please us, will outperform any whip-run dog who ever put a paw in a bird field. For folks, we're not going out for blood. Honest. We're going out for fun. To actually learn what a bird hunt is, please read my book, *How to Hunt Birds with Gun Dogs.* It's the joy of being there with your dog that keeps you afield. Not the bag. Anyway, the future calls for motivating gun dogs with love, not fear. And don't just speed-read over the above sentence, as well as the above paragraph. You bought this book to learn how to train a VSR and that is exactly what I'm talking about here. Right here is where I'm doing the training. Right here is where I'll be telling you how to do it.

WHAT THE DOG KNOWS TO BE A MAN

As the dog's bonded human partner, you will become the most important thing in his life. And he will respond to the whole aura of you (*now all of this is important*): his extrasensory perception (ESP) of you, your scent, voice, appearance, electric energy, the whole package that makes you—to him—the most distinctive and important individual on earth.

There is no one thing so strong between you and your dog as a bond. If not, then all dogs would be vagabonds who take up with you today and leave tomorrow when meeting someone new.

FAITH

What we're talking about folks is *Faith*, which is the Super Glue that holds all relationships together. Nothing else is so powerful, nor so important. You break the faith, you've lost it all. It's the rule with man and God, man and man, and man and dog.

Training with intimacy. This trainer takes time out to lounge with Chessie mother, one of her pups, plus two twin boys. The scene is placid, relaxed. That's the new way to train our gun dogs. No stress. No impact.

Why, Faith is even our collective name for the dog: FIDO. Remember, the root of the word comes from *fidelis*, which in Latin meant to be faithful.

I think we should reacquaint ourselves with what we have in a dog by reviewing Webster's dictionary definition of the word FAITHFUL: 1) "implies *continual, steadfast adherence to a person,* cause, institution, etc. which one feels morally bound to support or defend, 2) suggests *freedom from fickleness in affections* or loyalties; 3) implies such *strong allegiance* to one's principles or purposes as not to be turned aside by any cause; 4) stresses *unwavering determination...*"

And we would get a club and beat a dog that bonds like this? Or we would cast him afield and sizzle him with a charge of high-voltage, low-amp electricity? Or curse him with acid voice, and angered stance, and our brain in a heated meltdown?

CLYDE MORTON

Let me tell you two very important stories. Stories each of us should know and remember. Especially when training Pup.

Clyde Morton of Alberta, Alabama, became the most successful field trial handler the world ever, or will ever, see. He won the National Bird Dog championship eleven times at Ames Plantation outside Grand Junction, Tennessee.

Clyde's niece tells me, "Clyde was training one day and a dog just made him furious. So Uncle Clyde slid from his horse, stood there to get control of himself, walked to a big shade tree, and slid down its bark to sit on the ground.

I walked over and asked him, "Uncle Clyde, what on earth is the matter with you?"

And Uncle Clyde answered the teenager, saying, *"If I had touched that dog I would have ruined him. It's more important I control myself than control that dog."*

What Clyde was saying folks is threefold: 1) if a dog makes you mad he's defeated you; 2) you can take the spirit out of a dog, but you can't put it back in; and, 3) to let either happen is to break the faith and break the bond.

Now the other story.

A gal named Susan Butcher, just out of her teens, left Massachusetts and headed northwest seeking isolation; looking for the last wilderness. Her journey ended in Alaska, and single-handed she built her cabin, then gathered some sled dogs to get around. We all know to what end.

This gal in a he-man's world, Susan Butcher, became a three-time winner of the grueling Iditarod sled dog race. When asked how she was able to do it—all in a man's world—she answered (and I paraphrase), *"In a world where handlers generally felt they had to be tough with their dogs, I did it with intimacy and commitment."*

And what did Susan mean by commitment? She meant time. She meant taking each of these performance dogs into her life, into her heart and mind and soul, on a 24-hour-a-day basis. And if you aren't prepared to do that, you'll never have a miracle dog.

A NEW KIND OF TRAINING BOOK

So what you're reading is a new kind of training book for a new kind of retriever. Where we keep some of the old, adapt some of the new, but in all cases, point your dog to performance through love. Let me explain.

We know that during the past 60 years most dog training has been based on point of contact, repetition, and association. We put a collar around Pup's neck and told him to, "Come," as we stepped off. Pup naturally balked but we kept it up, for we had hold of him with our point of contact–the collar–and we kept repeating our command. We know what happened: the dog finally gave in. He followed us wherever we wanted to go.

Then we removed the collar and transferred our point of contact from the dog's neck to his ear drums (the verbal command had become associated in Pup's mind with the tug on his neck). We said, "Come on," and Pup followed us to the coop. Or wherever we were going.

LEAVING ALL THE DOG IN THE DOG

Now I've long been wondering why we need that collar and rope.

I've been wondering why we can't live with our dog, talk to him, give gestures and facial expressions and orchestrate our tone of voice, and adjust the chemistry we give off–until the dog understands most of what we want him to do–without understanding one American word. And we never tugged him once. We've taken nothing from him and consequently, by training this way, we've *left all the dog in the dog.*

Yes, I said chemistry! Are you aware the dog deciphers us many ways but knows us primarily through scent: he decodes all we are from booze to shoes?

Plus there is this: most everything a dog does–on his own–is related to peril, reproduction, and sustenance of life. Then further know that a dog especially triggers on butyric acid in deciphering threat in people, and be staggered with the reality that butyric acid is the primary component of human sweat…and man sweats a quart a day.

Therefore, the dog is decoding us by the millisecond with a nose so uncanny that you and I walk into a kitchen and smell hot tamales on the stove, but that dog smells cumin, coriander, oregano, chili powder, corn husks, onion, garlic, and on and on. Don't ever forget this. Never, Never, Never.

And the dog is just as uncanny in interpreting us through sight, touch, ESP, taste—Honest folks, Pup knows what we're going to do before we know ourselves.

So now I repeat: *we are going to leave all the dog in the dog.* And folks, we ain't done that for centuries. Let me repeat that: *henceforth we're going to leave all the dog in the dog.* Remember this. Don't ever forget this.

JIM CHARLTON

And this all-dog I'm talking about is the dog you'll have for your own when you've absorbed and put into practice the principles of this book.

For as Jim Charlton, the professional golden retriever specialist, in Portland, Oregon, says, "Why force the dog to do something? Give him time and he'll voluntarily learn to do it by himself." And that's what I'm talking about. It happens. And that's why I invited Jim to be a part of our group.

THE NEW AGE OF RETRIEVER TRAINING

Now across the nation there are several new developments in dog training duplicating themselves in the north, east, south, and west. It's evident we've got an idea who's time has come.

We now know every gun dog trainer should train more than one breed. This crossover training provides many novel insights and training breakthroughs adaptable to your primary breed. There are limitations in being a retriever specialist, a pointer specialist, a flusher specialist. This old way of doing things was so limited and repetitious and stimulus-bound.

We also know the ultimate gun dog is made by training with intimacy, not intimidation.

That ultimate gun dog must share your every waking and sleeping moment. We'll discuss this in detail, for the average wage earner

You'll be meeting Jim Charlton, the golden specialist from Portland, Oregon, later. Here he takes a pheasant from his ace, Sage.

now works away from home and home isn't a farm with land and birds. Home can be a huge city. We know. And we'll deal with it.

And finally, we now know we should keep our mouth shut, our hands to ourselves, and whistle Pup to performance. Yes, everything good that happens to Pup will henceforth be associated with the toot of a whistle. It's amazing what happens.

THE ELASTIC RUBBER BAND

The dog in your future will be a canine-you: sharing one brain, one soul, one heart, one intent. Think not? Then tell me how else Mike Gould of Kamiah, Idaho, has developed the concept he calls *the elastic rubber band*. Which you could well regard as empathy.

Mike casts his miracle retriever Web over the hill and without whistling him down—and for sure the dog can't see nor smell the handler—Mike walks forward and Web walks back. Mike turns left and Web turns right (they're facing each other). Mike backs up and Web comes in. Why? They're on the same wave length. And as I intimated above: dogs decipher ESP. They read our mind. And we never knew it. But we sure do now. Matter of fact there is no limit to what a dog reads. They predict earthquakes, foretell epileptics having strokes, sense people going blind and block their way before staircases. Yes, dogs are miracles in fur coats. And as miraculous as they are, you can get one at a dog pound for the cost of a dinner. Amazing isn't it? The only thing similar would be finding a mint Cadillac at the junk yard.

But before preceding you should ask yourself, how can Mike and Web do this? The answer is, Mike and Web have shared nearly every living moment of their lives together. So they have become one. And that's what you must attempt to do with your dog if you want the ultimate hunting partner.

We want dogs that when we itch, they scratch.

A HIGHER CLASS OF DOGS

We know, too, the Field Trial Champion no longer symbolizes what we want in the bird field. *There is a far greater Champion.* And that's the hunting dog: or in our case, the VSR.

Consider, the VSR has manifold ability compared to the field trial contender.

44

The training sessions of hunting retriever clubs are superb. It's the tests that are stupid and detrimental. Here the South Arkansas Hunting Retriever Club lines up at pond's edge to steady their dogs to wing and shot. Testy, huh! But remember, nothing can train a dog like another dog, or a whole line of them.

The VSR hunts all birds, not just pheasant and mallards. He learns their food preference, where they will be at any particular time of day, how they will react to him and try to elude his quest, and how they'll try to dupe him in their getaway.

The VSR enters every type of cover. He works outside the handler's sight. He uses his nose (as God designed him to do) instead of being a forced pawn in the hands of a trainer who directs him to and fro. He knows how to use the wind, and terrain, and bodies of water. He has learned how to adjust his hunt for dry or humid days, in direct- or crosswinds, in snow, ice, hail, or relentless heat. And he knows how to handle brambles and crisscrossed sticks and interwoven vegetation and fallen logs, and slippery rocks, and have the bank give way and drop him into a raging stream and sluff it all off as part of a hunting day.

45

Plus he learns how to pace himself, and avoid injury, and save his pads, and keep his nose clean, and doctor his eyes, and recognize rattlesnakes, and barbed wire, and sludge pits, and electric fences, and poison set out for coyotes.

The VSR knows all these things because you let him find them out by walking the fields together. He learned by doing it where the doing must be done, instead of faking it in some fabricated yard drill.

ER SHELLEY

For you see folks, Er Shelley of Columbus, Mississippi, was the greatest dog trainer of all time. But I now know one thing he invented that has hurt us a great deal and we must quit relying on it. And what is this fault?

Er's the first trainer to ever train on planted birds. He went to planted birds early in this century, since he predicted the world would dwindle, there would be limited land to hunt, bird populations would fall, and man would have to fabricate the field in his own back yard.

But I've trained with Er's apprentice, nearly-90-year-old Al Brenneman of Frankewing, Tennessee. (Incidentally, read Al's book, *Al Brenneman Trains Bird Dogs,* available from his home.) And what does Al do? *He trains his prospects on wild birds.*

Isn't that fascinating? Probably the second man in America to ever train on pigeons and today he prefers wild birds. That's telling us something.

The only training aids Al seems to have kept of Er Shelley are the chain gang and the pinch nerve to teach force retrieve. And we have, too.

WILD BIRDS

But you say, "It's impossible to train on live birds. I'm not a millionaire." Want to know something? That's the primary reason there are professional gun dog trainers. They have both land and birds. Otherwise, even they will tell you, why not train the dog yourself.

That's exactly what Rick Smith, living near San Antonio, Texas, and trainer of dogs that won 10 national Brittany championships, once told me.

46

And remember what Mike Gould said when I mentioned the average man doesn't have access to great expanses of land and wild birds–but he does. He told me, "Man's got to make up his mind what he wants in life. It's that simple. Stay in town and make money. Or move to the country and grub it out but have a life in nature where both dog and man feel they fit right in."

BACK TO THE HUNTING RETRIEVER

The new VSR, who is bonded in love, produces what you want because he wants to please you. The electrically shocked, beaten, or buckshot trained retriever goes through the motions out of fear. His heart's not in his work. He moves only to keep from being hurt.

These shock-trained dogs–we're really seeing the results in today's pups out of these electrocuted performers. These pups themselves, and these pups grown to dogs, are ballistic. They bound off the wall, they run amuck, they forbid training, they make every procedure a hassle. Why? Because their folks had to be Rambo tough, robotic if you will, to live. And now those mechanical dogs are throwing these unmanageable pups. I hear the same thing from nearly every trainer I meet.

THE BONDED RETRIEVER

The bonded retriever has the entire use of his druthers. If out of sight, the VSR just puts his instincts in overdrive and produces. The force-run retriever–when out of sight–panics and folds because his trainer has never given him any latitude. The dog has no idea what to do, but he knows he can't hide for he'll be found and beaten, and he sure can't go back without a bird for a beating waits him there, too.

FIXING THE FORD V-8

What I'm talking about here folks is an imperative I have for all of you now, and your sons (and daughters) who will train and hunt in the next century.

We want a dog with all the dog left in him. Understand? Up to now we've beaten too much of the independent performance out of the dog. The very independence that would (and will) make a better

47

hunter. *We've blunted the retriever's senses, limited his alternatives, restricted his movements, doubted his capabilities, and then cast this hobbled retriever to go hunting.* Remember the retriever who wanted the man to ride a unicycle?

How on earth can such a handicapped dog ever produce a bird?

Liken it to yourself. The foreman tells you, "Yea, go ahead and work on that car. But don't use your right hand. And for God's sake use only these five tools...not that entire tool box. And if you run into a snag come see me or read the manual. But don't ever go off half-cocked and think you can fix what you're doing by instinct. Always follow my signal.

"And oh yes. If you think you smell spilled gasoline or burnt rubber or anything like that, ignore it. Go using your nose and the people who judge me will think I don't have any control over you. Got me? We just can't allow such latitude in performing your job.

"And if you see something suspicious down the line don't go check it out. Leave that to us, the handlers. Your job is just to do what we tell you. Nothing more. Don't ever, ever try to do anything on your own."

See any similarity between the work this guy's assigned and the way a retriever is cast to retrieve at a classic field trial...and alas, it has now come to pass even at a retriever test hunt?

NO HARD HAND–NO MORE

What I'm saying is the age of dominance in dog training is dead. And if you get no more than this one fact out of this book you've got your money's worth.

Let's take a chapter to really nail this down.

Sitting Under the Gun Dog Tree

We'll make up a versatile shooting retriever
no test-hunt retriever could enter the field with."

Mike Gould has appeared in at least four of my ten gun dog books. He is a brilliant and innovative gun dog trainer, but more important to me, he's a sensitive, aesthetic, spiritual man who communicates with nature gods of rivers, mountains, plains, deserts—and when he talks to me about it, I listen.

I once taught a university course on the Folkways and Mores of Plains Indians. I've never known a contemporary man come closer to having that mystic brotherhood with nature more than Mike Gould. He is a 21st century white-eyed Indian.

Mike and I have been friends since that day we met in Alamoso, Colorado, to judge the first hunting retriever test ever held west of the Mississippi. Immediately we sensed we were two voices singing the same song, two shoulders carrying the same load. Light-years ahead of the dog training notions and practices of that time, Mike and I had separately learned dogs could read our minds, would respond best to mental stimulation—not physical repression—and would give maximum performance as the result of a bond.

THE GUN DOG TREE

Before Mike moved to Idaho, he had a big old box elder at his Carbondale place and we'd sit under its heavy-crowned umbrella and talk—I named it the gun dog tree—and we'd watch the sun come up, go across, or slide down.

49

Mike Gould walks a meadow beneath his beloved Mount Sopris at his Colorado game preserve. A bird boy tosses dummies as Mike steadies Lab at heel. That character holding two Labs in the back is Butch Goodwin, who you'll be meeting soon.

Our favorite time was dusk, when the sun would turn scarlet and cast jittering neon across the training pond. Trout would snap at the brilliant surface and sky-hunting bank swallows would make their final sweep before finding a niche to spend the night.

The last time Mike and I sat there he said in that low and measured way of his, "Bill, you and your writings, me and my training...we've tried to educate the public on what a hunting retriever is.

"I wonder if we've made a dent. Huh? I wonder if anybody has really understood?"

I answer him, saying, "Or if anybody cared?"

Mike chuckles as he says, "All during the retriever's history the scenario is played out where the hunter has already found the birds and already shot them.

"When what you and I want, is a shooting retriever. Not a non-slip retriever who casts only when he's released from heel. But a retriever out there hunting the cover and the lay of the land, knowing points of opportunity, knowing how to scent birds and then lock down hard to hold them until the gunner gets near enough to shoot. That's a shooting retriever and who the hell's testing them?"

What's there to say? If Mike weren't saying it, I would be. So times like this I'll study a bull bat making erratic aerials in the dusk sky, or hear the far-off kingfisher scolding the last minnow who evaded his dive, or just cram my hands into the soft cotton pockets of my jacket and cozy there.

After a while Mike says, "Any time people get involved with a hunting dog the natural parts just go sour. (Remember this when "natural trainer" Ben Williams takes us Hungarian partridge hunting later in this book.) They make dogs do false things at field trials. They make dogs do things that have so little to do with actual hunting, like running a blind after a bird the dog's not seen fall. I hunt lots of clients and I can add up all the blinds I've had to run on two hands. Know what I mean?

"Yet people will say, 'Oh, he's field trial champion X out of Z by Y.' And they think they've said something. Me? I'm thinking about one pot-licker I know. He's a pointer...he won't back, he won't retrieve, he won't come to you, he's kind of surly around other males, he's ugly as sin, he has a sad pointing style, but he pointed ten coveys for me one day when I was guiding in south Texas.

"What it amounts to is this dog has seen thousands of quail, thousands of coveys. And without the help of us at all...without the assistance of a trainer or handler...he's made himself a hunter.

"Now I run a big-buck operation here on this Upland Mesa game preserve. My clients want only one thing and that's birds. You and I might want beauty and poetry in the field and we may stand and watch a killdeer mother feint a broken wing to distract you from her nest or a spider weave a web...but these clients are business executives, their spare time is limited, and they want to take some birds home.

"So I'm not taking any "beauty winner" out there, nor am I going to take a field trial champion of any breed. I'm going to take a horrible old potlicker like that south Texas pointer who produces, and those executives will go home laden with birds and I'll have a sizable tip in my pocket. Then that old dog that's sinfully ugly starts looking beautiful.

51

"That's the problem. We as trainers...we as people...have gotten all screwed up. Somewhere along the line we started looking to what we as humans could achieve with a dog...the skills *we can help them attain*. What about the dog's own God-given skills? How about honing them? Or better yet, how about letting the dog hone his own?"

THE FIELD TRIAL AND TEST HUNT EXPERTS

There's a guy back east who called recently. He hunts with his retrievers and once tried to run them in test hunts. But that came to a screeching halt when he was not scored at a recent test. He asked the judge why and was told, "Because your dog hunted on the blind. That can't be done."

That can't be done?

This is not an isolated idiocy. I've been told one of the three hunting retriever clubs has an elected official who has informed the membership, and judges, no retriever will ever be permitted to use his nose on a blind.

If this guy actually exists, he doesn't want a retriever. Best he get himself a greyhound or borzoi or saluki. Such dogs hunt game by sight.

CONTROL

I really don't care if you can control your dog a half mile out on whistles and hand signals. Sure it looks good, but how does it figure in a bird field? What I want are versatile shooting retrievers. All that land the dog covers in running a blind is going to be disturbed earth, anyway. Land you can no longer hunt for the birds have likely flown or run away. The passing dog has disturbed them.

So why not go along with the dog and harvest any volunteer flyers en route?

Any retriever that hits the field hard, that knows where to go, knows how to lock the birds solid, holds them until you get there, watches the covey fly away, fetches dead fall, and relocates, is sure too valuable as a hunter to be spending his time running blind retrieves.

To Hunt Is Not To Run a Line

Mike Gould can cast his retriever Web to find a covey of blue grouse. When Web has the birds located he sits at whoa. Then Mike works his school of English pointer pups into the scent cone and steadies them on wing and shot. When Mike's ready, he can either ask Web to flush the birds, or he can leave them be. The point in telling this is: Web's power is holding those birds like their feet were embedded in concrete. Think of the power! With all that commotion of Mike training pointer pups. And that's what I want for me and for you. That power. And a well bred, and well developed retriever can have it!

So in this book we're not going to teach you how to score at some hunting retriever test hunt. Far from it. We're going to teach you...as we have been all along here...how to make up a hunting retriever no "test-hunt" retriever could enter the field with. Or better yet, let the retriever teach you, as he learns himself.

Our Breeding Program

It's dark now under the gun dog tree. A hog-bellied brown trout clears water and crashes flat-sided in the training pond. Mike piddles with a dry twig in his hand. Trying to peel the bark back with a ragged finger nail.

Finally he says, "You take the retriever trainers of America, we know most of them, they're good people, but they're out of control. They actually have no idea of the damage they're doing to their dogs, but also to their breeding program.

"You must always go back to Bob Wehle when you talk about breeding. Bob (the English pointer wizard) will agree, I'm sure, if a dog doesn't have brains, everything else you have is insignificant. Or the temperament: you must have something you can train and something nice to be around.

"This is what we're looking for. I'd rather have a dog with mediocre athletic ability and a great temperament, than I would an all-star athlete that's a jerk. That's not what my training clients are looking for.

"They want to take their dogs into the house, they want to walk in the park and show them off, they want them to be a part of the family. And when you start selecting breeders for some of those dramatic traits required for field trials, it's bound to cause problems.

"But you know what our really big problem is, Bill? You know the problem in getting the retriever recognized for all he can do, all he can contribute? It's training the hunter as much, or more so, than training the dog.

"Most people haven't thought of it, but just take the difference in game birds: their habitat, their nature, and their needs. With grouse you have one hunting plan, with pheasant you have a different plan, the dog needs to know all this to be a hunting dog.

"They're not born knowing these things. Which means we as hunters must teach them the basics. Take a dog that's a year old and has never seen pheasants, or grouse, or bobwhite, in their natural environment. The best thing we can do is get our gun and start following that dog and shoot birds for him.

"Just stick with the fundamentals, no flim-flam, good obedience, keep him happy, keep your attitude right, just show them everything about the bird and the field and the gun, and every single bird scenario you can imagine…and in their brain they just pile all that up and when they are four years old you get them out of the truck and they can take you bird hunting."

"You say it well," I tell Mike.

"Yea?" I wonder. "I've seen it all happen here in the Carbondale area. These people are moving in here from California and find out they can buy a hunting license and go hunting. But so many of them have never been hunting in their life. We concern ourselves about them having a trained dog and knowing how to treat him and care for him and hunt him.

"What about those people, themselves? They've got to learn to hunt, just the same as the dog. But more importantly, they're the ones who have to teach the dog. Interesting, isn't it? A real round robin, one depending on the other, and neither knowing what to do."

DESIRE TO CONTROL

"We have a fatal flaw in humanity," says Mike. That is this latent desire to control everything about us. Just realize, as soon as a king gets crowned he starts looking for somebody to kick their butt. Or take a democracy. A guy gets elected president and the opposition immediately starts looking for faults, and if they can't find any, they make some up to draw him out of his cover. So they can hit him.

"So they look for that one weakness. I think it's just human to control every thing."

THE DOG'S SELF DISCOVERY

"But this natural world you, and I, and our dogs live in–It doesn't allow for that kind of control. Nature ain't built that way. All control in nature is balanced. That's what makes it work."

There is a long silence. I say nothing. Mike offers no more so I say, "Well let's eat."

But Mike shows he isn't going to let it go, he says, "All training has to have something to do with the land and the birds. No other way will it work. I like control, too. I like my dogs to mind. But I don't want a dork out there. A guy comes up to me and says, 'Boy my dog did great over in Nebraska after pheasant. He took every whistle, he took every cast, everything I told him to do, he quartered beautifully for the whole weekend.'

"I say, 'Great,' but then I tell him, 'That's still inferior to the day you do that same hunt and never have to give one order to your dog. Never say anything to him.' "

Mike shakes his head as he says, "The farther you go in control, the deeper you get in prison."

"I know," I tell him. *"Ultimate training is no training at all... what's really important is the dog's self discovery."*

Mike smiles, he likes that, then stands. He brushes the dirt from the seat of his pants. I stand, too, asking, "What's for supper?"

"Spare ribs," I'm told.

Mike's groaning board proves, again, he does everything right. And as we leave the gun dog tree I want you to remember what was said here. We'll be training dogs a lot of different ways in the next several pages and then finally we'll go bird hunting with some gun dogs who never had a formal training session in their life. Remember. See which dogs you'd prefer to call your own. See which way of bringing a dog along would be the most fun for you.

Eight-week-old Scarlet fetches pigeon in unexpected snow squall.

Yard Training

*If you have little land and few birds you must
yard-train your VSR. It's a hard way to go,
but can be done. As proven since man moved
to the city and hired out for pay.*

How we yearn for 5,000 acres and tons of birds. For amber
vistas and big-domed skies with dust on our boots and wag-
tailed dogs.

But alas, man moved to town and left nature behind. So in
order to train his gun dog, he usually makes believe in a city lot,
using mechanical drills to pretend a day's hunt afield. And such a
skim-milk approach to dog training is possible as we shall see:
we've been doing it since the 1940s. But sometime—inevitably
sometime—that dog must be taken to the field to learn the joys and
pitfalls of nature and feel the fanatic compulsion brought about by
a bird. The ultimate VSR has got to have some of the cream.

So heed what I say here now. There is a whole new approach to
gun dog training. It has evolved from this writer and a handful of
allied and thoughtful pros—each member of the group inspiring
the other to take another step into innovative, no-pain gun dog
training—and the nature of the program is this.

The pup must start training the day it is born. I'll explain how
this is done later. Only minimally does the trainer give a verbal
command: 1) at no time is a pup asked to do something if he has
the opportunity to say no; and 2) a request is never made of Pup
when he's in a position to refuse.

But these two conditions are merely pre-stage. The imperative
in training the newborn pup is birds. Yes birds. I just stood at

Parker, Colorado, and watched 8-week-old Scarlet, a black Lab bitch pup, fetch a pinioned pigeon in an explosion of buckshot-snow scudding across frozen earth.

Scarlet knows birds, her handler, the words no, come, stay, leave it, and back. And then she doesn't know them. For they are often made known by whistle. I'll also explain that later. That is, Scarlet knows the whistle signals that mean all those things.

For this is the secret. Since Scarlet was born everything pleasurable that has happened to her has been associated with the whistle. The mother suckles, the trainer whistles (this is a Roy Gonia Special orange whistle). The trainer picks up Scarlet and loves her as he whistles. The bird is danced before Scarlet on the ground as the trainer whistles.

How long does this go on? Say six months. Remember this. Know this. Do this. Or some trainers say they want the dog to have it's permanent teeth. With permanent teeth, they believe, the dog suffers no discomfort in carrying a fetched bird.

So sometime around six months you and your own Scarlet start yard training. By then your Scarlet will know what all the commands are. She'll know the verbal commands as denoted by whistle signals, and most important, you will never be viewed as the heavy. You're Scarlet's helpmate, her fellow hunter, her lover, her feeder, her groomer, her bird boy. You're everything.

So now I'll go ahead and explain yard training as we've been practicing it in America the past 50 years. But don't you jump right into it. Wait for Scarlet to get older, wait until you've finished this book.

Wait! Yes, Pup will tell you when. Yes he will. When Pup starts to goof off, on what heretofore he was enthused about doing, then it's time to go to yard work.

Never start yard work first. It robs too much spirit and self initiative and inquisitiveness from Pup. Plus it can make a boot polisher. A dog who never leaves your side. Got it? Just present Pup countless walks about rich fields. Countless jostling experiences out hunting with whatever other pups you can mix in to a pack. Bring Pup to six months as a wild Indian. A wild hunting Indian. And then go to the restrictive yard commands.

For we can take the spirit out of a pup but we can't put it back in. And training Pup this way, he (or she) will always have that required spirit. There'll be much more on this when we highlight the dialog of two dog trainers each wanting the same thing, but going about it the opposite way.

HAVING SAID THAT

There are two traditional parts to this book. 1) We train Pup from seven weeks to six months with make-believe yard drills, which we'll do now. Then we introduce birds. 2) We take the dog to field and let him learn only birds. Then at six months we go to yard drills. Plus there is a third approach to training that I've converted to. Just take Pup to birds all his life and never have yard training. We'll see how that works, as well.

But whatever you do, absolutely do not start yard training with your pup until you've read the chapter on training Pup with birds. Please. *THIS IS IMPERATIVE. DON'T!*

WHISTLE TRAINING

To train with a whistle is a specialty of Gary Ruppel, Parker, Colorado, and a few others I've heard about but haven't met. The rule is everything **good** that happens in Pup's life is associated with the trill of a whistle. Pleasure/whistle. Good stuff/whistle. Happy times/whistle.

I don't mean a whistle that out-blasts a tug boat's horn. I mean a soft, nearly quiet whistle. A whistle that will gentle, tantalize, and seldom be used to force nor threaten. We'll have the amiable Gary take us through all of this. Just remember, everything good that happens to Pup will be reinforced with a whistle.

For it stands to reason: to give an oral command can be viewed by the dog as your being the heavy: there can be tell-tale inflection in your voice. Plus you're constantly talking to Pup and he knows that voice comes from you. So most orders should come from the whistle which is somewhat detached from you. For example, when Happy Timing, (walking the dog in the field) you're seen as Pup's friend and a giver of joy. To reinforce this feeling you whistle. For everything in the field is relaxed and easy going and nondirected. And Pup learns to associate this good feeling with the whistle. Thus, years down the road, the whistle to stop Pup in his tracks

Gary Ruppel fires up shooting retriever prospect with feather dance. Note whistle in lips.

(which could be viewed negative by him if it were expressed with voice) will always carry a pleasurable connotation. Know this, too, about the whistle. In the beginning Pup will naturally do many things wrong. And if you're constantly nagging him with your voice, what chance have you got? Because you want Pup to view you as the good guy and bond with you: love you.

Well, the whistle is not your voice. Save your voice for love, and your whistle for directions.

Admittedly, if you were walking Pup in the fields with eight other dogs, you would have to single him out by name if you had an emergency. A whistle would turn the whole pack. But that's only at the start of his life.

Later, working seasoned dogs in a bird field, a particular dog–under the situation he finds himself–will know whether the whistle is for him or for the pack. That's right. Dogs get that smart.

When Pup's five years old, he'll know the whistle means whoa, fetch, look to me for direction, stop sky-larking, quit trying to pick a fight, shorten your hunt, quit mouthing that bird, and whatever else you want it to mean. For Pup will automatically check what he's doing when he hears that whistle. And if what he's doing is something he's been taught is wrong, he will change his act fast.

Therefore, our whistle will not mean commands so much as: "Hey Pup, realize what you're doing."

But if you live in a high-rise, or condo, or you're centered within a 500-square-mile metro, oral commands are going to be a great part of your way of life. Heel, sit, stay, fetch, leave it, hie on, no, and come.

THE PUPPY

There are many truths in training. I've written them in many a *Field & Stream* column, several books, and pounded them home at seminars.

1. Nothing bad can ever happen to a dog he can associate with a human being.
2. Where ever a dog gets hurt, that place will always be associated with the pain. He'll never want to go back.
3. The best dog trainer is other dogs.
4. Dogs can be placed to self-train.
5. You can take the spirit out of a dog but you can't put it back in.
6. If a dog's made you mad, he's defeated you.
7. It's more important that you control yourself than the dog.
8. Pros know most dogs are best trained in groups: but there are exceptions to this. There are times a dog, or pup, must be trained absolutely alone.
9. You can never solve a problem without creating another. So it's best to never have a problem in the first place.

There are more truths, but these will do for now.

Nothing can train a dog better than another dog. The four Labs in near front are snapped to a chain gang while a trainer at field shoots bird for released dog. Lackluster performers on the chain gang soon say, "Hey Coach, let me in there."

The best way to train a pup is to live with him, to have him at side 24 hours a day (what Susan Butcher said was love and commitment). Impossible, you say? I know. That's our damnation for being city dwellers and working away from the home. It wasn't that way for the farmer, trapper, rancher, shepherd, free-lance gold prospector: remember? They could have their dogs at side for life.

Just yesterday I went for the annual wash of my 4x4. I walked the dog on leash into the office to pay up. Everyone started yelling, "Get that dog out of here...we serve food in here."

What they meant is they had a bunch of dried-out weenies on some hot steel rollers under a plexi-glass shield. I asked them, "Then how am I going to pay?" They renewed their bellers, "Get that dog out of here."

I left without paying and they had to catch me to get their money (which to their disdain was a free wash ticket). But I got to thinking as Pup and I drove away. There are 54,000,000 dogs in 34,000,000 American homes. If all those dogs are the bearers of filth and disease—as the personnel in this car wash (and the state legislature that passed the stupid law these people invoked) believe—then why aren't the occupants of those 34,000,000 households dead or diseased? Oh what an impossible world we devise when we're all huddled in the same human kennel. In Great Britain the dog lays under your table in the pub. In France every restaurant has its house cat. America's not very bright anymore.

Well anyway, the ideal is to have Pup beside you–and participating in your life–at all times.

I'll tell the story again of the young shepherd who had the journeyman dog. I watched the two of them work and was staggered with what this 8- or 9-month old border collie could do. So I asked the boy, "How on earth did you train him?"

And the young shepherd laughed when he said, "Train him? I'm no trainer. He just goes with me wherever I go."

SO HOW DO WE TRAIN THE PUPPY?

Ideally, we let the puppy self-train. It goes like this. Whatever Pup does that's pleasurable, then you whistle. But there's another set of circumstances. This is when you watch Pup and whatever he's doing you put a command to it.

You're watching TV and the scamp appears, bounding toward you. Tell him, "Come here Pup." When he sits to ponder what you've said, tell him, "Sit." When he leaves, tell him, "Hie on," "Alright," or "Back" which are three commands to do just what he's doing. Or, do all these commands with a whistle. Come here is one longer toot, followed by a succession of blips. You blow one blast for Pup to sit. And many handlers cast their dogs with two short pips of the whistle.

Now, should you think asking Pup to do what he's doing is a waste of time, then you've never tried it. Okay?

But know this: what you must have is a very bright pup. The difference in training a bright pup instead of a dumb pup is the difference between starting a Model-T with a crank and turning the electric ignition on your new Rolls pickup.

Two months ago a steel worker who took work out of town asked me to help with his Lab pup. I was told there was no way this pup could be house-broke.

Well, within five days this little guy responded to his name, the meaning of the word no, learned how to use the dog door, how to jump into the Trooper, how to settle in his crate and sleep without

This is Bob Wehle, the world's top gun dog breeder. Bob tells us his dogs do what he wants because, "They don't want to disappoint me." Bob is an early campaigner for no-stress training.

getting me up at night, and the imperative that he dump and tinkle only in the yard and not on the living room rug. He also became adept at fetching a tennis ball–but never releasing it.

In five days!

How was it done? Simple. I had seven other dogs in the house and with neither them nor the pup thinking about it, they showed the newcomer what to do. Plus I told our house guest to do whatever he was doing when he was doing it (sit when he sat, come

64

when he came, etc). Or in the case of tinkling on the rug…to stop what he was doing and get outside.

Also, I monitored this Lab pup all the time and took him out every two hours–plus each time I saw him rise and circle quickly, and after each meal (once again, commitment). I also took him to the same place in the yard each time, I stood and waited for him, and when he dumped or tinkled I praised him like he had just won some kibble-company's dog-of-the-year-award. And for me, and his steel-worker owner, he had.

THE DOG PROS

No human can train a dog like a bunch of dogs. Plus, this visiting pup I'm talking about not only had the benefit of the house pack but he never left my side for 120 hours. We were bonding.

Now let's consider the alternative. If I had but one pup and was teaching tinkle training, I'd be outside on my knees lifting the flap to the dog door and entreating the new pup to join me. But with seven other dogs rocketing through that door, the new pup's bound to follow.

Plus the other dogs dump and scent triggers Pup to do the same.

I also want you to remember everything that pup did to bring him pleasure was reinforced with a soft whistle. Never take your lanyard from your neck. It's the basis of all future miracle gun dogs.

When Pup dumps in the yard and you tell him what a great guy he is: whistle. When you serve his food: whistle. When you snap the leash on his collar to walk him around the block: whistle.

THE NATURE OF PUP

A pup (or dog) interprets his human partner through scent, hearing, touch, sight, empathy (or ESP), and taste. The pup is uncanny in decoding you; in learning what you are and who you are. His primary asset is his nose, but his other sensors are nearly as precise.

A pup (or dog) is very sensitive. Pups fold on pressure, but thrive on play and joy and love. That's one reason children make such good puppy trainers. So many times you must make your yard drills play to accelerate the pup's progress. Voice is especial-

I tell you not to turn your pups loose in high, abusive cover. But these little guys couldn't care less. That's the fire we want to see in all our gun dog prospects. And that's the result of good breeding.

ly critical to a dog. Yell and you've lost him. The good trainers whisper. The really good ones whistle. Women speak in a kind of giggle-voice and they do the best job of all. I've seen Bob Wehle, the English pointer wizard of Midway, Alabama, stand before his kennel of, say, 60 dogs, and whisper, "No," or "Stop that noise," and the pack falls silent. You wouldn't think they could hear him with their pandemonium in (say) seeing a strange car drive in. But they hear.

I once asked Bob how he kept them quiet, and he replied, "Because they don't want to disappoint me."

Bob knows dogs are uncanny interpreters of our moods. They know our anger and they know our happiness. And in all things they want a smile instead of a frown.

This becomes critically true when you and Pup have bonded. When you share one heart, one soul, one reciprocal empathic response. Like Mike Gould and the miracle dog Web, you can respond to each other as though, between you, there was an invisible rubber band. Or more precisely, a wireless walkie-talkie.

Or more than that! I'm thinking now of how dogs know what we're going to do before we do it. I don't mean something obvious like getting out a gun and therefore they know we're going hunting. They can discern this fact days ahead–while we're but thinking about it. We can tell they've decoded us by their actions.

But the only way this can come about is by you and Pup bonding. To do that you must live your lives together. I mean Pup's in the car, he's tagging along at the golf course, he's in the boat when you're fishing, he's at the drive-in movie, he's everywhere and anywhere you ever are, you ever go, you ever sleep, you ever eat or stool or work or lounge or play.

Now on with training–

THE YARD DRILLS

When Pup's learned the no-drip, no-dump, clean-house routine, you will go to the yard drill if you don't have acres of birds out back. But for Pup's sake at least have a live, piniened pigeon handy. You just can't bring along a gun dog pup without a bird.

Now if you did have that acreage out back, you'd never need any of these yard drills, you'd never need any gimmick training. You and Pup would walk those fields for months and he'd learn everything that you will ever teach in a yard situation…on his own!

BE CAREFUL

Be careful in starting your yard drills for this may be the first time Pup will view you as structured, stern, unyielding. Lighten up. Start your yard drills with play.

Throw the ball for Pup and let him chase. If he doesn't come back with the ball, so what? Go back in the house. Should he pick it up and run the other way, why not? Whistle (repeating soft trills) for him to come and if he refuses you, forget it.

But should he come running back with the ball in his mouth don't make a move toward him and try to jerk the thing away. If he drops it short, go get it, (or kick it with your foot), laugh, and tell him what a great guy he is. Pleasure-trill your whistle. Then give the ball a toss and let Pup bound out again.

If Pup passes you with the ball and heads for the alley, then whistle louder and turn about, running in place. Pup will think you're leaving him and come running. Pups always fear abandonment. When Pup passes you, reach down and stroke him, and tell him he's great. If he ever offers the ball, don't grab and pull. Instead, push the ball (softly) into Pup's mouth (to gag him), twist it (to loosen his tooth-hold), and remove it only to quickly throw it again. Never let Pup think you've controlled him nor denied him at this stage of his life. It's play, play, play.

Whistle, whistle, whistle.

FOR THE BIRDS

Now, I don't care if you and Pup live in a Manhattan subway tunnel. Now is the time you must get to the country and let Pup discover land and trees and water. Plus, let him find a bird. A dickey bird, if nothing else. Something that he smells and when he goes to look, the thing flies away. Hooray. We're starting a gun dog.

But this caution! Never make Pup walk in high or abusive cover. Always put him in nature he can handle (cover, terrain, moisture, stickers, etc). Plus the first encounter with wild birds could scare a young pup witless. So, though I continue to say you must train on wild birds, it's imperative you realize Pup's first bird has to be a pinioned pigeon. Something he can handle and man-handle.

THE DUMMY ERROR

Get a bunch of dummies and a collar and a leash and just keep repeating your yard drills and you'll have a mechanical dog with no fire, no curiosity, and no mission in life except to obey your featherless commands.

If everything Pup does pleases you, then he'll keep doing it. See? But should everything he does bring a scowl to your face then what the hell? Why even try. The point being you can take the spirit out of a bonded Pup with a frown: it doesn't take a whip.

Now for the Equipment

Apart from a wide vinyl, or leather, collar with a strong D-ring buckled around Pup's neck...that's snapped to a 22-foot nylon cord, say 5/8th-inches thick...you need no other equipment to train a pup. (Incidentally, that check cord must be thrown in a mud puddle over night, then dried in the sun for a day to give it the proper body to do all those things I ask you to do below.) Now Americans don't like that paragraph. America's present-day motto (based on the American present day penchant) is, "I can't do something because I don't have something." You know, "I can't go hunting cause I don't have the national champion."

"I can't go fishing cause I don't have a 22' Bass boat."

Well, all you and I need to train a dog is a bunch of penny-ante stuff you can get at any hardware store.

The Basics

Alright, we've attached a snap swivel to one end of Pup's check cord and tied a knot in the other: so it will catch our fist and not run through. However, know this. A knot can snag and really jerk a dog back and possibly hurt him. If the dog's running free, then let him have a slick rope.

Then we attached the snap-swivel to Pup's D-ring.

And I repeat, we will teach nothing here that Pup wouldn't learn on his own if he were hunting with you in the field. But there are many limitations connected with training on wild birds. Where do you get access to land? How do you provide the birds? What training laws are on your state statutes? Some of them are flat idiotic. They were drawn up by merchants and lawyers and not hunters.

You've got this anti-gun thing and some gal will screech to a halt and stride across the field yelling, "Killer, Killer, Killer." Tell her you're shooting a blank shell and she won't know the difference. And she'll probably yell, "Then if you're not killing them, you're harassing them."

And it's all understandable. Who knows country anymore? Who knows sporting arms anymore? Who reveres the hunt anymore?

We modern hunters live in a non-natural world where fallacies and stupidity are passed off as reality. Sometimes we are hard put to keep it all together. But we do. And we will.

Okay, on with the drills.

Gather up your check cord like a cowboy storing his lasso over his saddle horn. Walk along with Pup at your nongun side (we'll assume this to be your left).

When Pup's walking with you, stop. Whistle, "Sit." One long blast. Then step off, trilling, "Heel," and walk Pup some more before you tell him, "Sit" (whistle). And on and on.

STAY

When Pup's sitting and staying, toss your check cord out before you. Now put your left, flat palm down before Pup's face and tell him, "Stay"–or blow one loud, abrupt whistle note. Now turn a 180 so you're standing before Pup and facing him. Walk backwards ever having your palm up like a traffic cop, with your whistle between your lips, ready to blow, "Stay."

Should Pup start to come (and you can always read a dog's intent by checking his shoulder muscles–they must ripple before he can lift a paw) start toward him, whistling hard for him to "Stay." Note: the whistle is not the command here: it's your stance, your expression, your eyes, your dilated nostrils.

COME

When you get to the end of your rope (some 20 feet away) reach down, pick it up, and giving it a tug, trill, "Come." This rolling twill is always your come-in signal. And here's how it goes. It looks like this on paper –-, -, -, -, -, -. That –- gets Pup's attention, and the cadence of the stutters reels him in.

As Pup runs to you, gather in the cord (this goes faster if you guide the rope with one hand and milk with the other) to pick up the slack.

SIT

When Pup's before you, give a toot (long blast) to "Sit," then first clicking your fingers and making an arc near your left leg, you end up patting your left outer thigh, as you whistle for Pup to "Heel," which is one sustained toot.

After taking a break–letting Pup run about the yard and play–start it all over.

Only this time, when you stop walking and say "Sit" (the whistle will always be implicit from now on whenever I mention an oral command). Pull up the cord in your right hand, and push down with the expanded forefinger and thumb of your left hand–just before Pup's hips–as you tell him to sit. Sit he will (see photo).

Now when you're distant, ask Pup to come to you. Stop him in his tracks right before you and tell him, "Sit." Pup's facing you. Now reach forward, take Pup's two front paws in your hands, and pulling them toward you, tell him to "Down."

DOWN

Or, standing *beside* Pup and running the check cord between your heel and sole, thus making a pulley of your boot, pull up on the cord, which forces Pup's neck to the ground as you tell him "Down."

KENNEL

Then every time you go to enter a door, tell Pup "Kennel." And should you have trouble with this–because you've started too young, maybe–take Pup into the darkened garage at night. Leave the lights on in the utility room. Stand in the dark for a while and when you open the door to the light, tell Pup "Kennel." He'll be glad to escape from those dark spooks…especially if other dogs await him inside.

Mike Gould invented the power bar. It's a simple instrument that brings guaranteed success. Here Mike starts off with left hand clutching bar above solar plexus and right hand directing bar: tapping it, pushing it, tugging it. But never hitting or striking it so Pup is hurt or jerked.

THE RENEGADE DOG

If you are a pro trainer, you'll inevitably get in a two-year-old rowdy dog who doesn't know scat. Chances are you can obedience train with the slack check cord–but maybe not. You may need more fulcrum. So you'd use Mike Gould's Power Bar. Since we're training puppies there's no need going into the power bar here, but there is one aspect of its use we should know.

Bar is held this way for walking straight or turning right.

But when turning to the left, Pup gets "loose" on vertical bar. So bar is placed across trainer's lap and horizontal position bring proper control.

The power bar is a great instrument to teach sit and stay. Take your right hand and drop it low before Pup's nose. At the same time, raise up with your left hand pulling on Pup's neck. Also, with this two-handed motion, push both hands towards Pup's rear. He will sit.

Now to guarantee Pup stays, turn to face him and drop bar. Top of bar digs into dirt and angles up to Pup's collar. Now the trainer can pump the bar down with his left foot while he gives hand signal and oral command for Pup to stay (above). Then, backing away (below), trainer takes check cord with him, all the time monitoring Pup. But when trainer is ready for pup to come, he smartly lifts the top of the bar from the earth and saying, "Come," milks Pup into him—ever mindful not to let bar drop and dig into earth.

THE POWER BAR

For a dog the size of a retriever, the power bar reaches from your solar plexus to your groin. It's made of a piece of 1/2-inch conduit with a check cord fed through the barrel then looped at one end over a snap-swivel. Then the check cord is fed back through the hollow power-bar and tied off immediately at the bar's end. The remaining length of the check cord is thrown over your shoulder.

Now you snap the bar to Pup's welded D-ring. And away you go, essentially man-handling Pup with both your hands to direct him through his drills.

But where we want to use the power bar is to keep Pup sitting should he be breaking on us when we're distant. Have Pup at heel, toss your end of the power bar in front of Pup so the metal conduit wedges into the earth and angles up to Pup's collar (see sequence of photos). The check cord flies on further.

Now, taking the check cord in hand and backing away, we give the traffic cop hand signal and keep whistling pup to "Stay." If he attempts to move forward the power bar will jam him in place.

You can reinforce this as follows. As you're immediately in front of Pup and the power bar is wedged, use either foot to press down on the near end of the bar. This force will push back on Pup's collar and drive his rear-end down. Having done this, then back off.

When you get to the end of your 22-foot check cord you trill Pup "Come," and jerk the bar from the earth, milking the cord into you fast, so the end of the conduit doesn't hit the ground. Now, with the wedged bar, we can insure Pup staying when we're far away.

Should Pup try to angle around the wedged power bar, you'll soon become adept enough to lift the bar and throw it over in the direction Pup's going and wedge him at an angle. Hooray, we've got him (see photos).

HAPPY TIMING

All of this is laborious, dull, and self-denying for Pup. So we must intersperse our drills with a lot of Happy Timing–which is walking Pup in the fields. Letting him learn the country.

Pup's out there nosing up the toad, leaping sideways from the bull snake, rolling in cow pies, learning to infiltrate the multi-flora bush. And most of all, bumping chi-chi birds.

76

PLANTING BIRDS

Birds, birds, birds. There's no alternative, there's no substitute. There must be lots of birds. You can get them several ways.

One, ingratiate yourself with a farmer so you can dry-hunt (don't shoot) his land. Listen: the first time you visit a farmer don't tote a gun. Wear work gloves instead, and ask if you can help him do something.

Two, lease some land and hunt wild birds. Or ask your farmer friend if you can erect a Johnny house, which is a call-back pen for bobwhite. You release the birds when you arrive to train, then after you're gone, the birds call-back to the resident bird you left confined.

No resident bird, no call back.

And why the call back? Because bobwhite flock together, they like each other. Plus you've got food and water in there to make it all worthwhile for the birds to return.

Three, have your teenage neighbors trap barn pigeons in silos, flour mills, under bridges, in bell towers, wherever they congregate. Tote them to the country in a wire cage, transfer them to a game bag you can carry afield, and release them as needed. Or go to field in advance and plant pigeons by spinning them, tucking their head under a wing and planting them hard (wing-side down) or wing-clipping them, or hobbling them with a cord tied about each ankle and dangling to go through the nock cut in the end of a 30-inch piece of garden hose. So hobbled, the pigeon makes a slow flight where Pup is provoked to excitement as he marks the bird down.

Or four, plant your birds in an automatic, slow-release cage. Electronically you trigger this cage to slowly open far in advance. By the time Pup gets to the cage the pheasant's walked out and is hunkered down nearby. Pup will hunt him up and flush him.

RELEASE CAGES

Never, never, never put your bird in a pop-up release cage for a retriever. The dog'll work too close one day, leap to lock down the bird before it's been popped from the cage (either through a pulled string or electronically) and really hurt his face, his mouth, his nose. This cage is steel—we can't have Pup lunging into it.

Here's a slow-release (remote-controlled) cage with two wings open. Distant trainer presses button which triggers solenoid to open wings.

That's why we must have the slow-release cage so the bird's already exited by the time Pup gets there. The slow-release cage, unlike the pop-up cage, does not throw the bird in the air. The cage's wings slowly open and the bird looks around, knows he can exit, so he calmly walks out and stays close.

And realize, nothing can match nature in the rough: working Pup on *wild birds*. With wild birds, Pup learns their habitat, their location at different times of day, how they scent on dry days and wet, how they exit, where they go, how fast they go there, and on and on and on.

Direct Pup to wild birds in the hedge rows, the borders between row crops and natural grasses, where water meets a field, any place there is an edge. For you know 90 percent of all game birds are found within 10 percent of any edge. And realize, an edge is any change in cover.

Ensconced pheasant is not disturbed by slow-moving metal wings, so he bides his time, steps out of the contraption, and starts looking around for something to peck at. In other words, he's waiting for your retriever to handle him.

COVER

These cover changes can be subtle. For example, a plum thicket edges to a grass field. Birds will likely be there. Even if milo butts up against soy beans: the birds will be at this transition in habitat. An edge can even be the rough dirt of a pond dam scattering into grass; or a tight circle around a big cottonwood tree. Anywhere the topography, or cover, changes is where Pup must hunt.

And why is this? Because birds require some essential components in nature: an over-story of cover to hide from predators (especially hawks); bare dirt for the bird to dust in; short, thin cover to sift for insects and seeds; sparseness in foliage so the bird can make a quick escape (or mother bird can move her hatch without getting them wet from dew or following a rain); and open water for the bountiful mini-ecosystem that surrounds such oases.

This doesn't mean the birds drink surface water, it means they seek the seeds and insects that abound when water's near. Okay?

Well, we'll have much more to say about wild birds in a later chapter. But for now, realize we've run Pup through those yard drills that are essential for any breed of dog. These are the discipline drills: the drills that let us control Pup on a city street or a country field, or for that matter, in a house.

Plus, recall all these yard drills were conducted with a leather (or nylon) collar, a check cord, and a whistle.

Now we must bring in the hardware to continue. We must build the props that let us take Pup through the second phase of training. We've got to build structures, pound posts in the ground, string cable, and you must realize none of this is natural. You must realize if you could just stay afield with Pup, none of this hardware would be needed. But that's not an option for many of us. So get your hammer and spade and let's go.

But one hint as to the future. As to later in this book. There's going to be a mighty fascinating and informative debate between two professional gun dog trainers as when control must be instilled in a shooting retriever. Here we've just put the control in before hunting Pup. There's a trainer who'll "prove" this is all wrong. But on the contrary, there will be another trainer that assures us, "...it can't be done any other way."

It's all good stuff, you'll enjoy it. And you'll profit from it, mightily.

The Equipment Drills

*Steadying Pup on point with some two-by-fours,
nails, cable, chain, and rope. What ever happened
to the bird?*

You'll have to judge Pup's advancement: all dogs grow up different. Some may be ready for taxing drills at four months
(this is really an exception), and others not until they are 18
months old. Oh yes, I know all about accomplished gun dogs at 6
months. But I'll tell you later how it can be possible. At any rate, a
competent gun dog at six months of age is a rare event. And I
assure you, he is the product of an exceptional trainer with lots of
birds and varied land and cover.

And what are these taxing drills I'm talking about? They
involve the whoa post, the magic table, the chain gang, and other
advanced training aids.

THE MAGIC TABLE

There seems to be no limit to what you can teach on the magic
table. This is a large table, belt or crotch high, some 12 feet long,
and at least three feet wide. On each end of the table there's a
wood or steel stake rammed in the ground and standing at least
six feet tall. Stretched taut between these uprights is a wire or
woven cable. On this cable are trolleys with hanging snap-swivels.
Sounds like something out of the feudal ages, right? Something
you'd find in a castle basement. So don't let it be that for Pup.
Think, be cautious, be kind, when using this stuff.

Now we place Pup on the table, and with an intermediate chain or rope, snap him to the hanging snap-swivel. Pup can walk up and down the table—the trolley-swivel rolling along—or he can sit, or try to jump off.

If he jumps let him hang: there's never been a dog that didn't climb back up, and that puts an end to the jumping nonsense. Plus it builds self confidence. Don't be guilty of running to Pup any-time he gets in minor trouble. You'll rob him of self initiative and self resourcefulness.

Now we may put Pup up there for days, letting him get com-fortable. All the while we continue our yard drills: heel, sit, stay. Then we stand before Pup on the magic table and whisper sit. He does. Now we trill heel and start walking (we have a leash on his collar) and Pup follows.

When we get to the end of the table, we whistle stay. Pup sits or stands. Now we're not really teaching anything here, we're just getting Pup acquainted with this off-the-earth environment. For there is another law in dog training: take the feet away from a dog (a man, or a horse) and you've got him. Pup feels helpless up there and must get secure.

How You Want To Hunt Pup

Some hunters will want a VSR to delay-flush the birds. The rough-shod want a dog that'll just barge right in and erupt every-thing to the sky. A greater number will want the retriever to whoa before the birds and not move until ordered to do so. A lesser number, still, will want the retriever to point. And a few excep-tional trainers who can get all this taught, will want the shooting retriever to cast out at angle and loop behind the birds so he can drive them to the gun.

So you train for what you want.

I've always reveled in the zest with which a close-working shooting retriever locates the birds' scent cone, starts pin-pointing it's source, then in one tumultuous explosion lifts the birds to flight when the dog knows you're ready to shoot. Of course, this is best done in moderately light cover so you can read the dog and predict his action.

The way you teach this delayed flusher is to take him to tons of wild birds until the dog develops his controlled flush. It's the natural way.

Of course, those flushing dogs can only be handled by a person who can keep up. An older person, or one hobbled with ailments, might not be able to stay with the flushing retriever. Thus, all the birds would be flushed before the gun was ready.

However, you will read later about a trainer who doesn't care if the birds are flushed while he's distant. He primarily hunts a species of game bird where the whole covey doesn't erupt at one time, so he knows a remnant will be there when he finally arrives. Plus, he also learns from this flush at what elevation the birds are working, what cover they're seeking, what food they may be eating. Then he can concentrate in working his dog into "repeat" cover the rest of the hunt.

But for the guy who wants a whoaed retreiver, we can start teaching this on the table. So far as the pointing retriever, we'll deal with him later. Gary Ruppel will be our resident trainer.

THE WHOAED RETRIEVER

Keep working Pup back and forth on the table–hopefully having Pup jump, or fall off. Don't think he won't crawl back on: he will. Now he knows there's no way out. So you stand at one end of the table and pull Pup toward you, trilling "Come." But when Pup reaches the absolute edge of that table he's going to balk: he's going to stop. He doesn't want to fall off again so he's going to rear back.

Which means he's going to give you reverse thrust: like a landing jet. The more you pull, the more Pup's going to set up. So what are we teaching him? We're teaching him to be staunch on whoa. Which will later convert to being staunch upon entering the scent cone. We are in fact, turning Pup to stone on whoa before birds. Great!

So keep your check-cord tension taut, start whispering for Pup to Whoa, and repeat the command over and over, gently.

Which means, once again, we're telling Pup to do what he's doing.

Gary Ruppel has brought Lab pup to end of table and is putting on pressure with check cord. Pup rears back and digs in: in other words, Gary's doing everything necessary for a rigor-mortis whoa.

SYNCHRONIZE YOUR WATCHES MEN

Now this is important: all dog training requires split-second timing. Your commands must be synchronized with your physical action. As you say "Come," you Tug. Say "Sit," you push down. Say "Heel," you nudge. Say "Hie-on" as you thrust forward with a bowling ball toss of Pup's collar. Word and action together. Always together.

So a snap review: Pup's balked at the table's edge, but you keep increasing your pulling pressure on his check cored. So what does he do? He rears further back. In other words, folks, Pup's now applying reverse force to keep from moving. Hooray. Pup's whoa-ing with nonskid breaks.

84

When Pup's distant, Gary holds up traffic-cop hand signal and says, "Whoa."
Pup puts all four feet flat and doesn't move an eyelash.

We use reverse force with English setters who want to sit on point. We go to them and push down on their back with our flat palms. Their response is to push up. We keep pumping until we pump them to a standing position.

Okay. You keep telling Pup whoa (or produce a long, sustained whistle tone) as you tug his cord. The more you tug, the more he leans back and the more he resists. Now you got Pup whoaing.

SOON THE WHOA KNOT

Then finally, taking Pup from the table to the field, you keep him in place with a tossed whoa-knot (more on this later). Or you

85

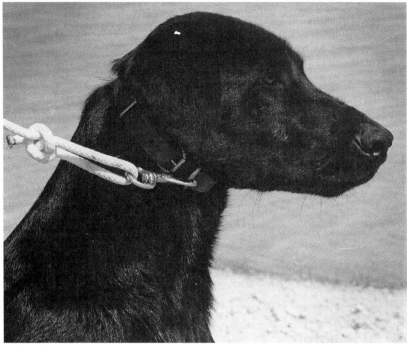

This good-looking Lab pup weaers a whoa knot. Its use will be explained later. But note: whoa knot is tied into check cord so when stretched out to front, it will be exactly opposite the end of Pup's lower jaw.

take Pup to the whoa post for an entirely different drill (tension now comes from the rear) which accomplishes whoa as well.

THE WHOA POST

This is a pointer drill that's adaptable to a shooting retriever. Here's how we do it. Outfit your retriever with two collars. Snap your 22-foot check cord to the forward collar. Now attach an 8- or 10-foot check cord to the rear collar Pup wears. This second check cord goes to a large post sunk in the ground. That's the whoa post.

Okay, take your 22-foot check cord in hand and tell Pup heel or alright or whatever you want (or two trills). Then start walking. Keep glancing back. Just when Pup will be stopped by the whoa post rope when he takes one more step, you whistle Whoa (one sharp, sustained toot). Your command will come at the precise moment Pup feels the whoa-post-rope tug on his neck.

Stand for a minute and let the drill sink in to Pup's mind.

Always do this with any drill: give Pup a chance to realize what's happened to him–and why.

Now release Pup to run in the fields for a few minutes, then return him for another session. This field-break is vital. If you keep Pup on the whoa post he'll tire of it, his tail will go down, and you'll lose all benefit of the training session.

I credit the whoa post to Delmar Smith, Edmond, Oklahoma, the horse trainer (who went to the dogs and made the Brittany a bird dog in America) and present-day gun-dog seminar host. I wrote a book about Delmar's training methods many years ago, and since then, I've been finding whoa posts all over America. Most everybody uses it today, and most everybody likes it.

What I want you to recognize about this drill is Pup self-trains. You're not tugging on him, the whoa-post rope is. So if Pup doesn't want to be tugged, he Whoas. Pup determines his own fate. Pup determines what he wants to endure.

STEADYING PUP ON A BARREL

There are other tools to help you teach Whoa. Most of them are made of stuff you can gather in a junk yard. You can put Pup up on a barrel with a cable running overhead. Snap his collar to the cable, then tease him with birds. What I call the feather dance. If Pup takes a step, let alone bolts, he can fall off the unstable barrel. Pup will learn to Whoa: to be steady, to put all four feet flat and not move an eyelash. Especially if you jostle the barrel or rattle the chain leading to his collar.

PUP ON THE FLY

You can even throw a rope over an elevated and horizontal metal bar, then push the snap-swivel under Pup's wide leather collar, thread it down his back, and wrap the cord about Pup's flank and snap it. You hold the off-end of the rope.

Every time Pup starts to move when tempted by birds, just pull your end of the check cord and pick him up. What'll happen is

Pup wears two collars. Each collar is attached to a check cord. One cord goes back to post stuck in ground. Other cord goes to trainer at side. So Pup is cross-tied. When trainer sees that one more step will tug Pup's rear collar, he says, "Whoa."

this. When you pull the rope, Pup will leave his feet and make a swing up toward your belt (you're standing to front holding the check cord). Hold him there a few seconds, then lower him back down. Since you've taken away Pup's feet he'll hate this. Pup will soon Whoa.

FORCE RETRIEVE

I've explained force retrieve in so many books I'd like to save our time and forego any discussion of it here. Plus the whole concept of "force retrieve" comes down to us from a heavy-handed past. I don't like the word. I don't like the concept. I do not want

Then trainer works to front, ever displaying traffic hand signal while he continues to tell Pup, "Whoa."

anyone to use pain to train a dog. And, most important, that Lab of yours has a great chance of becoming a natural retriever if you'll just keep shooting birds over him.

But for those of you who want a refresher course in teaching force retrieve let's have a go. The VSR is placed atop the training table we constructed to teach Whoa. You'll remember that table is belt- or crotch-high, some 12 feet long, 3 feet wide, and has a taut, over-head cable extending between posts sunk at either end.

You place Pup up there and connect the D-ring of his collar to a drop-chain. This drop chain has a snap-swivel on the free end, and a trolley of some description running along the cable. Let Pup settle, let him get comfortable and become familiar with the con-traption. This may be for three days.

Eventually, you take Pup's left leg and tie a 1/8th-inch nylon cord in a clove hitch just above the carpal joint—in other words, Pup's knee (see photo). Let the cord drop down over the front of Pup's paw. Circle the cord about Pup's two center toes. Bring the cord back up to loop through itself and form a simple slip knot.

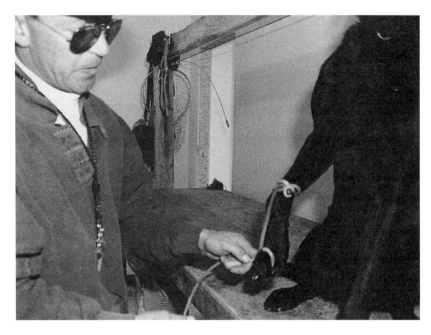

Gary Ruppel ties a clove hitch above Pup's carpal joint (above). The end of the cord hangs down over Pup's right-hand paw. Then cord is wrapped about two center toes (below) and looped over hanging cord. Some three feet of cord is left to extend beyond Pup's paw. IMPORTANT: Use cord as thick as possible so it doesn't cut into Pup's toes.

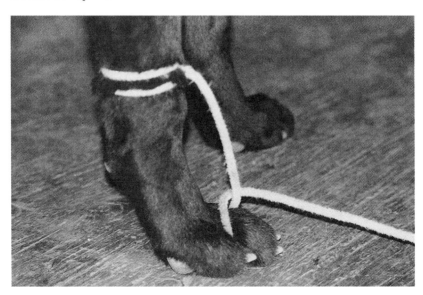

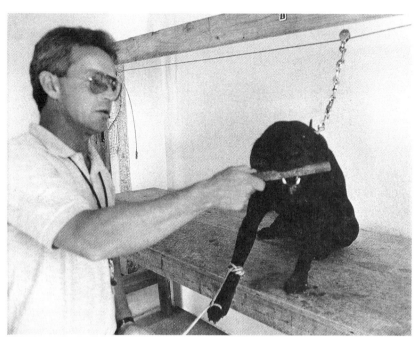

Gary works Pup with hard oak dowel so he doesn't bite down, which could later result in hard-mouth (above). The nerve hitch cord is pulled, Pup opens his mouth in protest. Gary places dowel between teeth and says, "Hold it." After grooming Pup's lips so they're not being pinched (below), Gary takes his right hand and places his fingers beneath Pup's collar while his thumb goes up into that cleft beneath Pup's jaw. This ensures Pup holds the dowel.

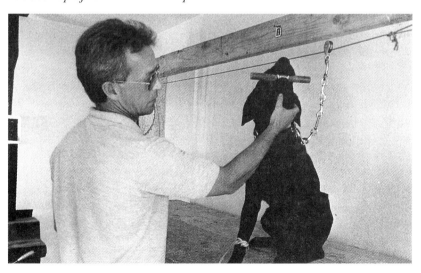

Now this cord is at least a yard long. When you pull the cord, it will extend Pup's leg, pinch the two center toes, and hurt like hell.

Why's that? Because we're duplicating the principle of placing a pencil over your middle finger and under the two adjoining fingers–then squeezing. What we have here is a *nerve hitch*: we're compressing a nerve. So the pain strikes us as unbearable (I've seen men go to their knees when military police applied such nerve compression and walked them to the door), but when the pressure's removed there's no memory, no imprint. If you've got to inflict pain, this is the most harmless way to do it.

Now why the pain? Because we want Pup to squeal and in order to do so he must open his mouth. And that's what we're after: an open mouth. Immediately upon seeing the mouth open, we plunk a retrieving dummy between Pup's jaws. He just made his first fetch.

Now let's expand our description of this process. Realize your left hand is pulling the nerve hitch cord, and your right hand is holding the dummy immediately in front of Pup's mouth so you can plop it in. When you insert the dummy you tell Pup, "Fetch." While Pup's holding the dummy, you tell him just that, "Hold it, hold it." When you take the dummy from Pup's mouth you say, "Leave it."

(Caution: there are three things you do while Pup's holding that dummy, or wood buck, or frozen bird. First off, groom Pup's lips so he's not pinching them with either his teeth nor the dummy. Two, grab Pup's leather collar under his neck with the bent fingers of your right hand, then bring your thumb up to insert in the V beneath Pup's jaw. This will hold the dummy in place. Three, having dropped the nerve-hitch cord, your left hand can now be used to love and soothe Pup's head and shoulders, groom his mouth to release any pinch on his lips, etc. All the time you're doing this, you coo to Pup and settle him down and congratulate him.)

When the dummy's removed from Pup's mouth, you walk him up and down the table (holding his collar) and let him shake it all off. When he's in a receptive mood again, you repeat the fetch drill. And you do this day after day (say no more than 10 minutes a day) until Pup becomes a fail-safe retriever. Tell him to fetch the kitchen chair and he'll go get it. Honest!

In the above photo Gary uses soft canvas dummy for fetch. He pulls the cord and you'll note Pup reaching out for the dummy. That's when you know you've got him. Finally, as you will see, fetching becomes an obsession. Below, Gary shows detail of lip and mouth grooming to be sure neither Pup's lips nor tongue are being pinched. Note, also, Gary's right hand as it uses collar and cleft under jaw to ensure Pup holds dummy.

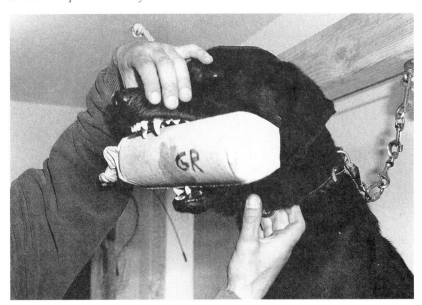

It's said Pup must be put through all this discomfort to assure us he'll never refuse to fetch a bird in the field. It's said a force-trained retriever never swims to the middle of the pond and refuses to take the duck to mouth. Or, he never runs a quarter of a mile after a strong, crippled pheasant and then blinks the bird, turns around, and comes back, leaving your dinner behind. They say a natural retriever always has that likelihood.

I wonder. I've had both kinds and neither of them ever quit me. You make up your own mind. But let me repeat. If you spend enough days, weeks, months in the field with Pup just going hunting, he will become a natural retriever on his own, and I assure you he will, over his lifetime, prove fail-safe. He will never refuse a bird.

THE HUMAN VOICE

Now something else. Traditionally there have been all kinds of oral commands in yard training. But try not to take them to the field. Why is that? Because your incessant chatter will distract Pup: will break his concentration. So keep quiet unless you must save Pup's life by booming, "No," or if your wife's along and you don't want her to see Pup rub in a cow pie. After all, Pup's sleeping in your wedded bed and some women can be finicky. If she sees Pup in that cow pie, both you and Pup'll be sleeping in the dog house.

THE DOG THAT WON'T GIVE IN

Now a strong self-willed Pup can be obstinate. He can flat fight you on that table. So you may need to nail him to the wall. That is, put a U-bolt in the wall, run a rope about Pup's flank, and cinch him up. Now he's tied by collar and waist. I've even seen pro trainers with a renegade dog chain the dog to a second trolley and literally pick up his hind legs to elevate his back paws so they merely skim the table. Now the fight may not be taken from him, but his capacity to sustain the fight sure has. He's yours.

And again, I repeat, I hate all this wrestling and conflict. For Pup knows who's pulling that cord; he knows where the hurt's coming from. And he's looking straight into your face. Want to break the bond? Seems a mighty good way to do it. Therefore, I'd much prefer Pup become a retriever on his own—just by fetching up every bird you shoot. And he will. Once he figures out that's what pleases you. Once he learns that's what you want.

GROUND TRAINING

When table training is finished, you place Pup on the ground and repeat the whole process. Incidentally, you leave the nerve hitch cord wrapped about Pup's carpal joint—but not around his toes. Pup runs and the cord flaps behind him. Now all you've got to do to jog Pup's memory is reach down and tug the cord. Or, using your boot toe as you say, "Fetch," just tap the carpal joint wearing the cord and Pup's incandescent will snap on.

DUMMY SEQUENCE

While you're on the table, you switch from dummy to frozen pigeon to live pigeon. Then you do the same thing on the ground, and you're done.

Why the frozen pigeon? Because we don't want Pup to become hardmouthed, and he won't bite down if that bird's frozen—a frozen bird hurts his teeth, same as it would yours. Also, if any trainer sees Pup smashing the canvas (or plastic) dummy, then he immediately replaces it with an oak dowel. Oak's hard to imprint.

Also, when you take the dummy from Pup's mouth and say, "Leave it," you push; you don't pull. That's right, you gag Pup by pushing, while at the same time you twist the dummy to break any tooth hold.

If that doesn't work (and it usually will), then blow a sharp blast of air up Pup's nose. And if that doesn't work, then reach for that flap of skin that runs from Pup's back leg to his lower waist, and hooking a finger under it, pull up. Pup will drop the dummy since you just hit another nerve.

I will say this about the force-retrieve table. Whenever a dog goes off his game or seems to forget his commands, then you return him to this table and go to force retrieve, and it's amazing how he shapes up in every respect. Of course, that's true with any form of discipline. The same thing happens if you return a dog to yard drills. You'll be amazed how fast they seem to remember everything and their whole body language shouts at you, "Let's leave this place and get back to the bird field." As pointer people say, "Once again you've got your dog in pocket." "Out of pocket" is their way of telling you the dog's gone amuck.

WHOAING ON PLANTED BIRDS

You can use a dummy to train a retriever to fetch a duck. However, I've seen young, naive pups enter a derby or started retriever at a field trial or test hunt who had only trained on dummies. When the dog reached the floating duck he barked, leaped sideways, and pumped back to the casting line with a lot of white showing in his eyes as he glanced back at the infernal critter that waylaid him.

UPLAND GAME

My point is, you can't use a dummy to train a retriever to hunt upland game. He's got to have stimulation, he's got to have frenzied confrontation, he's got to have a bird fighting for it's life to arouse all the sporting blood in the dog.

One thing a versatile shooting retriever doesn't need, and that's marking drills. Marking drills are only for dogs who enter the field after the action's passed. With our Pup, he's the source of the action. He's there from start to end.

But I say this, and then I must say that. Later you'll read a discussion in which it is contended that marking builds confidence in the dog. The dog is not taught to mark so he can fetch–though that's what he does–he marks to gain more assurance about everything he does. You read it all and you decide.

I do not agree, because once again we're asking the shooting retriever to hunt by sight. That's what a mark is: the dog "watches" it fall. I want the dog to essentially find birds with his nose, not his eyes.

THE BOBWHITE

The ultimate upland game bird for a shooting retriever–the one that excites Pup most, is probably the easiest for you to handle, and gives both Pup and you the greatest outdoor thrill of your life–is a wild bobwhite. We've all seen our retrievers knock up a pheasant, and we've mentioned how Mike Gould uses each year's hatch of blue grouse to train his starting pointers after his miracle Labrador, Web, locates the covey.

Most game birds are easily brought to wing and shot with a retriever (there are exceptions and they will be explained), but nothing, nothing, nothing that flies on the face of the earth will wind you and Pup's fiddle strings so tight as an exploding covey of bobwhite. This is the ultimate hunt with a retriever–a hunt I've made hundreds of times with Jim Culbertson and our joint packs.

So bobwhite hunting is how I'm going to teach you to approach a game bird, teach Pup how to hunt, how to honor a scent cone, how to work the bird to either slam him down or continually relocate to keep him available for your gun, then honor wing and shot, and mark both deadfall and covey relocation.

Let's get birdy now.

Steady to Wing and Shot

That backyard of yours with the garbage can,
clothes line, jungle gym, and barbecue just
doesn't stimulate Pup like a lespedeza patch
loaded with wild bobwhite. You'll see that now.

Finally there comes the day. The day Pup meets the liberated bird. Not a wild bird but a liberated bird. That magnetic mystery in the bush that dilates his senses, stops him in his tracks, and sends a million years of instinct hurtling through his brain.

For you've outfitted Pup with your 22-foot check cord and started walking him in a prepared field. Which means you've mowed sections of the cover but left tufts or stands where birds can be secreted. Or you've hauled in limbs and stacked them in a tumble, so you can push a hand deep inside and hide a bird.

You're walking into the wind and getting close. You know where the bird is hidden. All your attention is fixed on Pup. Look at him! He's not got it yet. Whoops, no that's not it. There he has it. Look at that head thrust out, the rear knees cock, the planted front feet, the forward set of the ears. He's baffled, and yet he knows. He knows he's been here before: what was it, 10,000 years ago. For it's in his genes. He knows. Look at his flanks tremble.

Tighten your hold on the check cord to hold Pup in his tracks. A bumper winch on a Suburban wagon couldn't be more definite. Should you let Pup break now, *that's what you're teaching him. Remember, whatever happens to Pup in training is what you're teaching him.*

Don't grab Pup's check cord to jerk him back nor distract him. When Pup's on birds he turns into one 50-pound nose. Let him savor it.

99

Bird boy shows hobbling device that gives Pup both a planted bird and a long, slow escape flight. Pigeon has two ends of same cord tied about ankles. Cord is threaded through nock in piece of discarded garden hose.

When Pup is whoaed, start walking forward, going hand-over-hand down the check cord. When you get to Pup, kneel down (I'm assuming Pup's to your left-hand side). Anchor your left knee to earth, your right leg bent, foot flat. Your left arm goes around Pup's flank. Your right hand grasps his collar. Your right elbow is bent and tucked into your side for rigidity.

You say nothing! Remember: nothing, nothing, nothing!

Now think about this hold you've got on Pup. He can't kick out from the rear, can't lunge forward, can't duck and go under your body then scoot, can't twist his head out and jerk loose. But know this: a full-grown pointer can (it feels to me) just literally jerk your arms out of their sockets. Except for Chessies, most retrievers pump a little less iron. But you hold on. I've seen lightweight trainers drug across the field like a sliding anchor.

THE BIRD BOY

With a nod of your head, a bird boy appears from nowhere. He walks to the planted and hobbled pigeon, reaches down and lifts

100

Trainer has walked Pup into scent cone and now anchors him as detailed. (Note: in this instance, handler is left-handed.) Bird boy walks forward and lifts garden hose, giving whoaed and anchored Pup a feather dance.

the off-end of the rubber hose. The pigeon comes up flapping: yes, Pup's feather dance.

We've got to take a break. That hobble! Here's how you make it. Cut a three-foot section of 1/8th-inch cord. Get a section of discarded garden hose about two feet long. Nock one end. Poke the cord through the nock and tie so you have two equal hanging ends. Tie those two ends to the pigeon's two ankles. Do it so there is no impediment of blood flow. To display the bird, lift with the off-end of the garden hose while the bird flies.

Okay, the boy raises the pigeon high, it flies above his head to dart here and fro. The boy starts hurrahing, just making this demonstration the most exciting thing Pup's ever seen. You say nothing. You don't move. Then the bird boy casts the pigeon to

101

When Pup is frantic with desire, bird boy launches hobbled pigeon to wind and Pup marks spot of relocation.

sky as he yells, "Boom," or whatever. Only later does he actually fire a training pistol; later still a shotgun.

When that bird is first "danced," Pup will want it. He'll whimper and lunge and twist. He'll froth and jerk and leap to paw the sky. But when that bird is launched, Pup will suddenly know he was born to be an astronaut.

Incidentally, Jim Culbertson and I never did any of this to steady our hunting retrievers on bobwhite or any other upland game, nor do we now. I'm explaining this for those of you who can't bring your retrievers along naturally and must depend on drills and pen-raised birds.

I was just afield with Ben Williams of Livingston, Montana. Ben's a 40-consecutive-year-breeder and trainer of long-legged prairie Brits. Ben's pups never see a pigeon. From the day they start going afield they are trained exclusively on wild Huns. Everybody wants a Ben Williams Brittany.

Don Sides of Coffeeville, Mississippi, displays proper "right-hand" anchoring of Pup before planted bird.

MORE ON THE HOBBLED BIRD

Now the vital thing here is Pup must have enough latitude to watch the fly-away down. If you can get him to watch the flushed bird go to earth, then you can check-cord Pup to this new location and hold fast as he honors the new scent cone. And one important note: some purists say Pup can't move or turn when the bird's launched. They say that exhibits a dog loose on game. Bosh! If he didn't move or turn, how in the hell could he watch the bird down? Some people just don't know anything about hunting birds.

And realize this–that bird does land, and land fairly soon, because he is toting the weight of that garden hose.

And what is this sign Pup gives that tells you he's making game? Let's repeat, for you must learn to read your dog. It's a

103

tremor, a frenzy. The ears cock. Pup looks more intelligent than a Harvard scholar. This is fact. Pup flat looks smart. Then his nose is extended, the ruff on the back of his neck may rise. His tail can do one of several things, depending on the dog. The tail can quiver, not wag. Or it can go flat still, extended like a skillet handle. Or it can beat like that metronome that keeps rhythm while your kid practices piano. Depends on your dog. But that's the point–you learn your dog's signs. That's part of bird-hunting a retriever.

One hunter told me he always knew if his dog was certain he had a bird pinned down. If the dog's mouth was closed, the bird was there. If the dog's lips were parted, the bird had left. This is one example of knowing, and reading, your dog.

Sometimes the dog looks back in a plea that he either be released to go get the bird, or you get your rear-end in gear, or you just flat shoot. Remember those eyes. *For Pup's telling you that bird is there and I want it.* He's telling you, "*I know what I'm doing…are you sure you do?*"

Therefore, as much as possible, you don't want to draw Pup's attention to you. And that's why–if you must give a caution, or command–you "Psssssst," or soft-whistle (even spit-whistle if you think about it). Just a hush of air between your compressed lips. A whistle that the guy beside you may not hear.

Remember: a whistle is always associated in Pup's mind with something pleasurable. That's the way he was raised.

And what other reasons are there for these faint sounds? Because the ordinary sounds of man can spook a game bird before you're ready. (Ever seen a field of pheasants launch when you slammed the pickup door?) Plus any loud sound will distract Pup. But he'll endure a "Psssssst" or a whistle trill. It will settle him, it will cock him even more for what's coming. It will tell him he's doing good and that you're on the job, and will verify for both of you that you're in bond.

WE'RE NOT TEACHING WHOA

Remember, we're not teaching whoa in the bird field. Whoa is taught only in yard drills, on the magic table, or at the whoa post. What we're doing here is introducing Pup to birds in a controlled situation. Matter of fact, and this will jar your mind–*whoa has*

Students of a Delmar Smith dog-training class check-cord pointers into scent cone. Note taut ropes. There's power ther.

nothing to do with birds. Whoa is not even taught with birds around, remember? Whoa means for Pup to put all four feet flat to earth and not move an eyelash.

Also think of this. Should you have said whoa when you went into the ground anchor—and Pup broke—then you'd be guilty of a training fault. *Because you never give a command Pup can break.* Or if you say whoa and Pup takes a step, *then that's what your teaching him.* To creep on game. So no verbal commands will ever be spoken around birds.

Think back of all the guys you've hunted with who were an incessant chatter of "Whoa" and "Watch it" and "Steady there..." when working their dogs on birds. Strange how so often we naturally do the opposite from what's right.

Also, *you never want to put Pup into a situation where you have to say no.* Pup steps forward and you bark, "No." Now you've put him down before birds. What's your next act to destroy a good dog?

So the whoa has got to be in the dog, not in your command. Whoa has got to be in Pup in a structured situation that he knows about: which includes you, the wind, the bush, the bird, the scent, the

105

gun, the approach. That's why yard work must be completed before you ever go to the bird field. Pup must know when whoa is needed. You don't have to tell him about it. *For you'll remember our first requirement in picking a pup: he must be intelligent.*

Something else, how many hunters do you know start piddling with Pup on point? They raise his tail and brush it up. They lift him off his hind legs and bounce him up and down. They run their fingers against the lay of the hair…their hand going up Pup's back. You know what all that nonsense does? It distracts Pup and makes him loose on game (anyway it does a VSR). So not only do you keep quiet, you also keep your hands to yourself.

Now many great gun dog men groom Pup up on birds. Fine. That's their prerogative. I just advise you not to do it. And these grooming-on-point guys all say the touching tells Pup he's doing well, that rubbing the fur the wrong way staunches him up even more, that it's all a reward.

Pup knows exactly what you're thinking 100 yards away. Pup read our minds. Pup knows you are pleased. You think staunch and he'll get staunch. You don't need to touch him. But you choose the way you want to go. It's your life and it's your dog.

And just as soon as I say that I'll say this. Mike Gould of the Flying B Ranch has 12 Elhew pointers in his string of 55 dogs. And while Mike's working them, I continually see him stroke the tail up, run his fingers against the grain of the pelt on Pup's back.

And I must admit the dogs settle. It seems soothing. But do we want settling or soothing before birds? As far as I'm concerned, keep your hands to yourself. In all the years I've hunted gun dogs I've never rubbed one the wrong way.

STOPPING AT THE EDGE OF THE SCENT CONE

Now why did we stop Pup at first scent? Because we don't want him to crowd the bird. This is especially true if you ever take Pup to a game preserve to hunt for store-bought poultry. Those hot-house birds will let Pup get so near…that if he duplicated this distance on wild birds you'd have a wild flush.

But consider this. The retriever's job is to find the bird, it's usually the hunters job to flush the bird and shoot. But yes, many retrievers are hair triggered—mine always have been. And they will flush game...you just have to know how to read your dog and know when feather's coming up.

Now that I've said this, then I must also say the opposite. Ruffed grouse may be our most wary upland game bird except for mountain quail. But do you know ruffed grouse can be successfully approached and taken to bag by a VSR? It's being done. But the VSR we're talking about here is one of two: he's either a pointing retriever or he's a whoaed-flush retriever. He's not a flushing retriever. Or, and this is always the case when it comes to a dog exercising supreme caution, the dog may be quite old.

RETIRING THE BIRD BOY

After many anchor drills, feather dances, and frenzied lunges by Pup, we send the bird boy home. Now we preplant the bird ourselves, get Pup out of the car, and check cord him into the bird field.

Once again, when Pup hits the edge of the scent cone you tighten your check cord. Only this time you do not go to Pup and kneel down to anchor him. Instead, you give a soft whistle (one distinct note), or make no sound at all, to turn Pup to stone. Then you start walking a *wide circle* about Pup, heading for the site of the planted bird.

Now why the wide circle? Lots of reasons.

Let's say Pup's made game and you're certain where the bird is hunkered down. Then why not walk straight to it? It's not done. Let's say you walk past Pup—who's making game—and catch your pants leg on a supple limb that whips back and cuts Pup's face. There is a real possibility you just made Pup man-shy, cover-shy, and bird-shy. And should the bird flush when the twig snaps back and you shoot, then possibly Pup's also gun-shy. Hooray! You just set your training schedule back six months, or maybe forever.

So never, never, never go near Pup when he's whoaed before birds.

'Cause I ain't told you everything yet.

Listen: do you know why that bird is sitting there instead of flying? I call it predator power. Power like you've never seen before. You don't know what it is. I don't know what it is. No one knows what it is. This power of a gun dog.

It's that thing between hunter and hunted. Like that night in Korea when I heard the bolt slide back and slam forward to seat. I whoaed. I strained every sense. I didn't breathe. I later realized that's just how that bird feels before Pup. It's why the whole thing works. C-O-M-M-U-N-I-C-A-T-I-O-N.

The presence, the essence, of that dog **welds that bird in place.** Otherwise that bird would fly. It's that simple.

That dog is sending a message. It says, "I've got you." And the bird knows it. The bird knows he's going to die. That's the way it is in the wild. That's the way it's always been. Will always be. *Everybody's somebody's lunch.*

Let's get to where I was going.

If…you…don't…walk…a…long…way…around…that…dog… on…whoa…then…you…may…walk…between…hunter…and… hunted. And when you walk between dog and bird, the power is broken. The power of that dog paralyzing that bird to sit is broke. And that bird can fly away. So that's the main reason you never walk between a dog and his bird. But let me say this: a VSR usually works so close to the bird there wouldn't be room for you to walk between them.

Back to training.

THE WHOA KNOT

Here's another training device: and it's very important. Incidentally, you don't take Pup and run him through every drill I outline. Maybe one or two drills will instill all the control you'll ever need.

Plus, as Pup responds more favorably to one device–say the magic table–it might be you're pitiful at pulling it off. So both of you must concentrate on those drills that do Pup the most good and are the most efficient for you to handle.

Okay, here's the whoa knot. It's tied in the check cord an inch behind the front teeth of Pup's lower jaw. How's that? Well the snap-swivel is snapped to Pup's welded D-ring. Then the cord comes off toward your hand. So where that cord is an inch behind Pup's front teeth, that's where you kite a bowline knot. (Check your Boy Scout Manual on how to tie this knot.)

Should Pup move on whoa you flip the check cord and send a shock-wave of force down its length to whomp Pup under the chin with the knot.

Shock wave travels lightning fast down check cord to whomp Pup under jaw with whoa knot.

Your command "Whoa," or better yet, your one abrupt whistle tone, must come at the precise moment the knot bumps Pup's chin. This throws Pup's head up and breaks his concentration so now he must start thinking all over about breaking Whoa.

And why must the head go up? For Pup will always lower his head to run. Don't all sprint runners leave the blocks with their heads down?

Now this is imperative. The whoa-knot drill demands the knot bump Pup as the command Whoa (or whistle tone) is heard. Practice. Have a friend tie the check cord about his wrist and hold his fingers up, palm flat and facing out, so the whoa knot bumps his extended fingers at the precise moment he hears your command. Got it? Only when he says you're synchronized can you start to train.

THE WIDE CIRCLE

So now you're walking out there in that wide circle, constantly monitoring Pup, and should you read he's thinking about stepping forward or breaking, you let the whoa knot zing. Read? Sure, you see his shoulder muscles start to tremor.

Same thing's true after you reach the bird's location. You're directly facing Pup and have complete control through your check cord and whoa knot.

Now reach down, lift the nocked garden hose, give Pup the feather dance, and launch the bird to flight. Watch Pup! Does a muscle ripple in his shoulders? Get ready. He may break. Be quick with the knot. But what's this? He's holding. He's actually holding. And are you proud? Does the sun shine in Arizona? And Pup's proud, too.

Remember, Pup has the same emotions as you. He grieves, he laughs, he hurts, he sulks, he desires, he seeks. Whatever you can feel, he can feel. When you finally know this fact, it will help strengthen the bond. For when you see Pup display a feeling, go with it. What you're seeing and interpreting is genuine and you're on the right beam.

PUP'S EYES

And I've saved this until last regarding your reading Pup. Everything will always be in Pup's eyes. Learn the eyes. They will tell you everything. Think not? That's the way Pup reads you. Have you never marveled at how an 8-week old puppy knows to look into your eyes? How does he know the eyes see? How does he know the eyes communicate? Why else would he be looking there? It's a fantastic world, isn't it?

BACKING

I've never taught a hunting retriever to back. These dogs just have an uncanny sense of working with each other. If the lead dog needs help, then the other dogs will supply it. If he is best left alone to work the covey, somehow the other hunting retrievers understand this and leave him alone.

To teach a pointing dog to back, the following rules must be instituted.

A dog backs by sight, not scent. The instant the trailing dog sees the lead dog point, he Whoas. And a trailing dog can either be behind, to side, or to front. The pivotal thing being that this

110

Veteran pointer handler Tom Smith of Edmond, Oklahoma, watches Pup at end of check cord to see if he's going to break on lofted bird. Note Tom's right hand is poised to send shock wave if shoulder movement is detected in Pup.

dog is not directly in the scent cone and has not established the first point.

Should the honoring dog move one foot on whoa, here's what you do. Silently you go to the dog, physically pick him up, and return him to the exact spot he vacated.

Remember, I've told you dogs are very aware of place. They know exactly what you're doing.

Repeat this often enough and the honoring dog will get the idea and hold to Whoa.

The consequences of non-Whoaing on back are many: there can be a dog fight; the lead dog can be distracted, break his power and the covey escapes; or the lead dog may break point and move forward and therefore become loose on birds.

So always insist the whoaing dog Whoas, and that means, he puts all four paws flat and doesn't move an eyelash.

RUNNING SLICK AND FREE

Now we take our VSR to field without a check cord. He's running free. Once again, we've planted birds in likely objectives,

111

and we're working Pup into the wind to better help him find these planted birds.

Whup. There he's got it; he's sliding to a stop. His nose searches now, quizzing the wind, trying to pinpoint the precise origin.

You say nothing to Pup. You walk away from him, far away, and go in a great circle to the bird. Once again, you lift the bird and launch it. While doing this you are very mindful of Pup, watching his shoulder muscles to see if they move and thus tip you off he's going to break.

If he does, an abrupt whistle blast should weld him in place. But Pup stays and you would think this has been a successful session. It has, but there is more. In order to tighten Pup up on point (or standing or sitting at whoa), we need to produce another bird. Here's how this goes. If you produce a single bird and loft it, fire a gun, and let Pup watch the bird fly away, that's fine.

But realize Pup is ready to chase that fly-away bird. He's always got this on his mind. Consequently, as he's enduring juvenile pain because he can't chase, you produce another bird, fire, and let it fly away, too.

Has this got Pup to thinking? Could his thoughts go like this: Are there unending birds in that grass? Could it be if I stand here long enough I might be released to chase one?

No, that never happens. But as each successive bird is produced, Pup becomes more all-pro. He's relaxed, though staying tense enough to do bird work. The stress is gone, but the desire remains. Now we've got Pup feeling good. He stands competent for bird after bird. He says, hey this game is starting to look good.

There are professional trainers who will tell you that in the beginning Pup may break point and chase these flyaways. That's part of their wild Hunting Indian routine. But I don't extend my Indian options that far. *You cannot correct a fault without creating another one.* That's another Tarrant law of dog training: why create a fault in the first place?

These pros will tell you, "Oh well, I can take him off chasing any time I want to." Maybe they can, but not without consequences. To correct any pup for any problem can be severe and painful and demoralizing. I don't want that for our Pup. I want him (or her) to continue burning high octane, with all their chrome polished and set on ready with power steering.

This retriever backs English pointer on bobwhite plant. If retriever moves, handler will pick him up and carry him back to the exact spot he vacated. Remember: dogs are very mindful of place.

Now when hunting Pup on wild birds (never taking him to yard drills, never presenting him in a structured situation to planted birds), yes, you can let Pup break and run. That's how Momma-dog would be teaching him if she had the job.

But this is an entirely different set of circumstances. Most puppies will self-break of chasing birds once they learn they can't catch them.

All this wild bird training is best taught in a pack. Then one day Pup decides he wants to chase, but he looks about and finds himself alone. So he wonders, why didn't the rest of them run? And it's all self correcting.

And actually, the pack approach to dog training is the best, but who has the kennel room, the food budget, the kennel wagon, and all the rest, to be running a pack of dogs? That's why I emphasize

113

one-dog training drills and techniques. One dog comes closer to representing our reality.

Okay, we've taken Pup to field on liberated birds and, thus, staunched him up on game. Pup whoas now, honors wing and shot. So let's move on where we can put Pup on wild birds and see the added zest that emanates from his work.

The call of the wild is as exhilarating for Pup as it is for us. But there'll be a slight delay in getting where we're going. The reason is threefold: 1) we must explain that you can't fire 12 gauge shells from a .410 (that is, no matter how gifted a trainer you are, or how hard you work, you can't make a miracle gun dog out of a dork), 2) we must first whistle-train a pup so we can see how that works and what's accomplished, and then, 3) we must train a pointing retriever.

When this is done I think we'll have the essentials to go to wild birds. Okay?

✳

Breeding Determines
Success in Training

*Gertrude Stein grew famous in her Paris literary
circle by writing, "A rose is a rose is a rose."
If she'd written, "A dog is a dog is a dog," she'd
have been thrown out of our huntin' rig. Because
there has never been, and there never will be,
two dogs alike.*

We're going to whistle-train with Gary Ruppel now and he's
going to make some statements like: "This humane training
that I give these dogs *would not be possible if we didn't have a much
better class of dogs than ever before.*"

He explains, "If we had the old bonehead, snarly, self-willed
dog of yesterday, we'd still be out there heavy handed."

Our breakthroughs in training are attributable to better breeding. That is, producing dogs that are biddable, who take to training easily, who desire to please, who seek human companion-
ship, and seemingly have an innate sense of knowing what's right
from wrong.

Take the typical old English pointer. He carried a ton of carnal
instincts. He'd bolt, chase a deer, wipe out a coop of chickens, kill
a couple of cats, and bore on until he was picked up three coun-
ties away.

But today's English pointer, especially as bred by Bob Wehle of
Midway, Alabama, seems to come from the womb genetically
trained and predictable. So much so that Bob Wehle, two years

ago, showed me the pup named Snakefoot, and said, "Bill this is going to be the best dog I ever raised."

The outcome? Snakefoot won the National Shooting Dog Championship, then turned around and won the Masters. In June, Snakefoot was declared the National Shooting Dog Champion for the year.

THE WRONG SIGNS

So know this: if a dog ducks his head from you with white dominating his eyes and sulks back if he thinks you're going to reach out, it's unlikely you'll ever get a bird with this dog.

Or, if another dog is snarly and snaps, you're in for a time of it there, too.

I just had a dog in for training that had cold eyes. I'd tell him no, and he'd give me a threatening look. Or he'd comply when I told him no and he'd stop what he was doing–only to be back ten minutes later doing the same thing. This dog was destructive, quarrelsome with other dogs, perpetually nervous (as displayed by chewing and digging), and sought me out only to please himself– never to please me.

In other words, bad breeding had produced a bad dog and more important, good training isn't going to correct it.

GOOD BREEDING PRODUCES GOOD DOGS

On the other hand, since good breeding more often produces good dogs, you've got to know your bloodlines, how they mix, and who's getting the job done. At the same time, you've got to know these dogs that seemingly come trained from the womb* aren't the rule, they're the exception. Not everyone has them for sale. It's a small and select minority. What I'm saying is the immortal champion is one dog in a million. As I've written

---

Dogs coming trained from the womb are an impossibility as you know, but dogs with the propensity for easy training are now the product of good breeding. Like I've said all along, you've got to be able to read the dog, in this case the parents, to know what you want in Pup. Which means, further, that you've got to have years of experience. But which one of us didn't start out raw? It's the way with everything you want to do in life.

Author ponders newborn pup and another three weeks old. When females are kenneled together a long time, they start to cycle together. Thus, the pups almost have the same birthday.

numerous times before, how to pick one? I wouldn't know. Therefore, I spend my time praying, not picking, hoping God will give me the miracle dog.

Now this doesn't mean two backyard pot-lickers can't throw the VSR of your dreams. I've had it happen. But it happens with more regularity—more well predicted, let's say—among established breeders who have established track records.

What I'm leading up to is this: the retriever you need for upland bird hunting is the intelligent, biddable, fanatically birdy pup some breeders are whelping today. You can take a lackluster, lazy, disinterested, half-bright retriever through yard and field training and end up with a ho-hum sort of gun dog, but not the one you and I want.

To get that DOG-OF-A-LIFETIME, the pup must come with brains, temperament, and desire. And only momma and daddy

117

can put that in there...and these mommies and daddies are in the hands of breeders who know what they're doing.

This dog I'm talking about with brains, temperament, and desire...that's the dog we must have to train on wild birds and have minimal yard drills. Anything less in a dog and he'd be bewildered with the complexity of you and the bird in the field.

THE SHOCK-TRAINED DOG

Let me say this: avoid at all cost the sons and daughters of electrically shock-trained dogs. Such pups are too often bone headed, obstinate, extremely nervous—all because their sire or dam was trained with brutality and pain rather than sensitivity and love.

You see, a shock-trained dog performs only to avoid pain. He is a grudging victim and a resentful worker. The reason he can stay in the field (and this predominantly means field trials) is he has the constitution to take punishment and not crumble. But that same resolve to preserve no matter the pain, makes a dog self-willed and begrudging to a human.

You should also know this: these dogs know they must perform only on command, never having an independent thought of their own. Why, they can't even use their nose to smell a bird as we saw up front. Consequently, when these dogs are out of sight, they are out of control; they run amuck.

The loved-trained dog, however, exists and performs with extreme self confidence and wide personal latitude. He's loved to excellence. When the love-trained dog goes out of sight, he just turns on four-wheel drive, puts a different disk in the computer, and proceeds to get the job done that he intuitively knows you sent him to do.

So, stay away from shock-trained dogs or get the misery of your life.

THE OLD DAYS

A hundred years ago when most people lived on a farm, old Momma-dog, with her distended belly and heavy teats, would one day disappear from the house. Then about four months later she'd come back, leading a litter of six pups.

An Elhew dam stands to shed herself of suckling family.

If you took one of those six pups to the field, you'd discover the most amazing thing. Momma-dog, by herself, with no assistance from any human trainer, had taught all those pups to hunt, point, back, and fetch.

Those six pups knew cover, where game would be at any time of day, what way the wind was blowing, how to run without drifting off the slope of a hill. And they'd learned it from a dog, in the wild, over birds.

And how well were they getting the job done? They all had full bellies when they came to the farm house.

This teaches us something, doesn't it?

So, what we're going to do in this book is go on, now, from the imitation-trainer (that is, a man or woman who attempts to imitate

119

Wehle honks goose horn to entice pups to follow him about fence.

in his back yard everything that Pup will encounter in the bird field) and we'll just take a raw pup and head for the back 40.

I know of no better way to do this than with Gary Ruppel's training technique.

GARY RUPPEL

So meet Gary, the soft-spoken, deflective, mild-mannered, humane gun dog trainer—you'd swear he should be an intensive care nurse—as he tells us how he prepares a retriever for the bird field. Then we go Gary one better, and together, you and I take Pup afield to train on wild birds.

I'm a desert rat freezing in a Denver snowstorm, and with the thin blood it takes to withstand a 115-degree day, I'm cold but my heart's warm. Scarlet, an eight-week old Lab puppy, is lifting a big, wing-clipped pigeon from the frozen earth and coming toward me on side-angled legs, fetchin' a bird as big as a pterodactyl for her, fetchin' it to hand.

Eight weeks ago Scarlet wasn't even alive. Five weeks ago she couldn't even see, and now she's fetching. Makes you wonder about all the grown dogs that don't know scat, doesn't it?

This is the most important part of this book. Here's where we build the versatile shooting retriever.

WHISTLE TRAINING

Mike Gould is the training guru in America today. No one is more brilliant and innovative. Years ago, when Mike was running a big-buck shooting preserve at Glenwood Springs, Colorado, he learned his friend, Gary Ruppel, had hurt his back as a cabinet maker.

Mike went to the hospital and told Gary he wanted him to manage his kennels: you know, clean up, look for illness, take care of everything. That was Gary's break.

From scoop shovel to training genius, this 40-year-old, slightly-built, soft-mannered, gentle-voiced guy has revolutionized puppy training in ten years. Mike's apprentice has now become a force in his own right.

How? Simple. It's his attitude. Gary says, "I'm the kind of guy who hates it when somebody doesn't like me. The dogs come in here and I see the look in their eyes: they're saying, 'You're a jerk.'

"I don't want those dogs thinking that way. I want them loving me. I want them looking at me, saying, 'What's next?' And that's what started the softness with me."

HERE ARE THE RESULTS

Gary has two specialties: training puppies and developing pointing retrievers. Let's look at the puppy program.

He says, "I don't want any of that natural desire stifled in a pup or a dog. Why would you? You've got a dog that's capable of going out there and giving you a show in the field, and if you stifle that with hard-core obedience, with total dominance, that dog is never going to be able to express himself.

"I tried that dominance route, and I didn't like myself for it, and the dogs didn't like me for it, either.

"So even before a litter is born, I start blowing the whistle. Just a soft trill, over and over. I use an orange Gonia special whistle. You can get them everywhere.

"And even though those prenatal pups can't hear nor see, I believe they can feel those vibrations of the whistle.

"And when they open their eyes, and they can hear, I really start to emphasize the whistle, just to get them used to the noise. And so now they're moving around and that's when I really start handling them. Pettin' them, lovin' them, cuddlin' with them. And the whistle goes on and on.

WEANING

"Then when I wean them, that's when the whistle really starts to take over. Everytime I bring that one feed pan for the whole litter...I use a stainless steel pan...I clang the thing on the cement. Make lots of noise. Get the pups used to noise. Later it helps in making a dog that's not gun shy.

"And what's happening here is the whistle is being associated with the pleasure of food. That's the key. Always the whistle means pleasure.

"So now I get the whole litter outdoors, and we go for mob-squad walks. What you call Happy Timing, Bill. And I'm whistlin' all the while. A little guy drops back…I whistle. And here he comes. They're coming on the whistle. And that's the most difficult thing to teach a pup. If they're interested in something else, why would they come to you?

"Then while we're out walking I lay down on the ground and let the whole litter explore me. They run over my face, stick their tongue in my ear. They learn I'm their buddy.

THE PINIONED BIRD

"Now, at six weeks I get out a pinioned pigeon. All the while I'm still whistling. Bird/whistle. Food/whistle. Pleasure/whistle. Then I teach sit. Mike Gould calls it the Oscar Meyer syndrome. Say sit, or blow the whistle, the little guy complies and you give him a piece of weenie dog.

"Then when they are 8, 9, 10 weeks old, I teach them to turn on the whistle in the field. I just take fun walks with that pup, and if he's to my right I correct him with my physical movement. In other words, as he's going right, I go to my left. Then he looks over to see where I'm at. I'm blowing that whistle and going left, so now he turns and goes left. He's just taken his first direction signal, and he doesn't even know it.

"I really pour on the praise: you know, good dog, good dog.

BIRD BAG

"But something else I do is this. I carry a bird bag, and when that pup's going left, I throw a bird so the force plants itself and head right. Now, when that pup turns and comes running toward me, he enters that bird's scent cone. So what does this mean?

"It means that every time that pup does what I tell him in the field, he finds a bird. Now you got a dog that handles and believes in you.

"But…and this always happens…sometimes, inevitably sometime, say at 9, 10 or 12 months, that dog is going to refuse the whistle. You're going to blow it and he's going to say, 'Hey I'm doing something over here…knock it off.'" And that friends, is when you go to yard training.

123

"But when you go to yard training, now, you're taking a wild (but controllable) Indian. You got something.

"It's then you go through all the stuff that you explain with the hardware and the training drills, Bill. The whoa post, the magic table, the chain gang, all that stuff.

"And that's all right. You know it? I'll tell you why. In yard training the dogs have to do it. Because you're asking them to do it. That's part of their job.

"We feel like we take good care of our dogs. We take them to the vet. We feed the very finest food on the market. We let them sleep in our beds…they are part of our family. That's our job to love them and care for them.

"But they have a job, too. And that's to come when you call. To stop on the whistle. So we enforce that in the yard.

"But we don't stifle the pup in doing it, because we put such a big motor in him during his first eight months. He's got the motor, he's got the gas to run it, and he's got the desire to please you. You're on your way to making a versatile shooting retriever."

A PRO FOR THE FUTURE

I told you Gary was something special. He's the wizard at training with love and tenderness. All those good things I've been preaching for twenty years. We'll be hearing lots about Gary, and from Gary, in the years ahead.

Now, Scarlet's a jewel, but I'm not saying we should all have an eight-week old Scarlet, the wonder pup. Too many bright prospects have been burned out by lesser gifted trainers than Gary. Also, there is still this: just bring the dog along naturally, and in three years it may be that both your slow-processed pooch and Scarlet are on the same level, but no Scarlets are possible without land and birds. Scrape that with a stick in the fresh concrete of your kennel pad.

But before that, remember, Gary has another specialty, and that's the pointing retriever. So let's take a look at this new development in retrieverdom. Is this what you want in the bird field?

※

The Pointing Retriever

*Americans always seem to have a fad. At this
time, for some bird hunters, it's the pointing
retriever.*

I pull into Gary Ruppel's diggin's outside Denver, Colorado, and
find him emptying frozen kennel buckets. He hails me through
a billow of mist and I can see the ever-present smile, even behind
sunglasses. Gary always wears sunglasses.

"How you doin'," I ask. And he hollers back, "It's another great
day God made for the dogs…and you and me. It couldn't be better."

Gary means it. If you aren't training gun dogs, to Gary's way of
thinking, you aren't living. It doesn't matter if it freezes, or the
kennel roof is blown off by a tornado, or the whole lot of his dogs
come down with kennel cough. Just being with the dogs will sustain Gary through all this and more.

Gary's been in the gun dog business ten years and knows more
than most who've been in it forty. Gary, and whoever else is like
him, is the future of gun dog training, because he loves dogs, he's
experimental, thoughtful, and he's content to be just what he is
and not try the stock market, or a hamburger franchise, or part
ownership of a car wash.

Mike Gould, of Kamiah, Idaho, who took Gary out of a hospital to manage his game preserve kennel, says, "A trainer is not
going to learn much from field trial prospects. Those dogs can be
the cream of the crop. Where he's going to learn is from the scum
bags, the run-off artists, the biters, the fighters, the guys that want
to climb the fence and run away, all that sort of thing. Taking in
pit bulls or whatever, that's how you learn to train dogs.

"And Gary is like me in the sense he needs money, so whatever dog comes down the road he takes him and trains him. Consequently, Gary has learned how to train."

Incidentally, Mike has a book coming out on shooting retrievers, *Title of Mike's Book,* from this same publishing house. Don't miss it.

I've talked often with Gary about his softness, his humane training, his self-imposed requirement that all his pupils love him. Piece by piece he's revealed, "As a child I went to Catholic school for eight years. A school taught by Franciscan nuns, you know, a Holy order named for the saint who loved animals. And those nuns instilled that love of animals in me. I never thought once of becoming a dog trainer though...or working with animals. But when it happened it was the most natural thing in the world...like that's what I'd been prepared to be, all along."

He pours me a plastic cup of coffee from a bullet-shaped thermos bottle, and I pour a bit over the rim so I can touch my lips to it. I ask, "Got any pointing retrievers?"

"Yea," he says with slyness in his voice, "I got those rascals."

"You're getting good at training them, aren't you?" That's not a question, that's a statement.

Gary waves me off saying, "If you can call it training."

"Well the word's out you're the best," I tell him.

" I heard the same thing about you, Yoda," he says.

"Ohhhh, hooo," I yipe and spin around and almost swash out my coffee. "You goin' to one of those win-friends courses?" He doesn't answer. "Or you practicing on going into politics?"

He still doesn't answer, but the first time Gary called me Yoda I said, "Yoda? What the hell you talking about?"

And he said, "You know Yoda, the guru in *Star Wars,* you're my Yoda."

"I don't know *Star Wars,*" I told him. "If it ain't of this earth, and gun dogs, and bird fields, and guns that don't jam, I know nothing about it. I've never seen a *Star Wars* in my life."

"Well, your Yoda," repeats Gary as he points to the third kennel run down the front row. He says, "There's a pointing retriever. Want to see him?"

"Come a few hundred miles to do it."

We take the dog to field and work him on liberated quail. He does point; he backs; he honors. A man could shoot birds over him. I ask, "How do you train 'em?"

"I start all retrievers as pointers," he says. "That is, they go straight to pointing training. Of course I put them through my whistle-conditioning program the first nine months if I have them as pups, while at the same time I'm exposing them to birds.

"It doesn't matter whether it's wild or tame birds," he points out, "just as long as Pup's not put down by either one. By that, I mean it's tough to train on wild birds with a pup because his legs are so short. He's running against stubble or tangled grass or twisted brush tangle."

Then Gary surprises me by saying, "I don't care much for pointing Labs."

"What?"

"They're fad dogs," he says, "A product of popularity and ego. America's like that, you know. Wants something different; something unique. Why, you and I come up with a purple Lab with pink spots and we can retire."

"You're right, but what's the big deal, anyway? I've seldom seen a young Lab who wouldn't point a hen pheasant. It's just in them to do it."

"Yea, that's an impulse point, or an instinct point. But what we're talking about now is the trained point for a retriever, and some can do it if you help them.

"You know, the natural dog," says Gary, "the dog in the beginning of time...would get close to the bird, figure out the situation, find the exact location, then pounce on it for dinner.

"Later, man taught the formal pointer to stay way back. To point at the edge of the scent cone. That got the hunter a lot of spooky wild birds for his game bag. But these Labs don't know that. They've not been genetically directed toward that. It's like starting all over at the beginning of time for them."

God, I love it when Gary or Mike or one of the other bright young trainers devise another way to bring along a gun dog without pain. I'm always exhorting them to move onto the next plain of gun dog training, to throw off the dead hand of the past, to be innovative, to think. I know it's not fun pushing them all the time, but the *dog* is the beneficiary. No dog should ever feel anything more harsh than a disappointed look on his human partner's face or a loud voice. That facial expression and that voice

Labrador retriever looks down in point on planted pheasant.

can hurt a bonded dog more than a whip-run dog who's hit with a two-by-four.

THE SIGHT POINTER

By now Gary has gone to his kennel truck and released another dog. He says, "What most people don't realize is these pointing retrievers don't scent point, they sight point. They enter the scent cone, walk forward, point, and while they're doing that...because they are so close...they are generally looking straight down at the planted bird.

"Oh yes, it's vital to say 'planted.' For you know the pointing Lab came about due to the game preserve movement. These pay-as-you-go operations with liberated birds are everywhere in America today. And those tame birds hold for a close point. Those are not wild birds. They don't explode at a dog's encroachment.

128

At different camera angle (above), pointer appears on film as Gary kicks out pheasant. Lab gives chase and Gary does not fire to encourage break (below).

Well, that fits the pointing Lab's mode. He's crowding the bird; he's standing right over them, looking down.

BACK TO YARD TRAINING

"Now, yard training is mandatory to develop a pointing Lab. He must do what you tell him. Say 'Whoa,'and he must stop. That's the most important part of it: the dog's manners.

"Now, a whistle-trained pup grown to a nine-month old dog enters yard training with a free sprit, self assured, highly motivated. Everything's gone his way, he's happy, he's alive, he's curious and bold, and now he's got the thrust in him to see him through repressive yard training.

"So you put a check cord on the retriever and walk him into a planted bird. If he doesn't whoa when you tell him, or if he doesn't stop to flush, then you've not done your yard training well. Go back to the basic drawing board.

"While I'm working on planted birds, I also put the dog on the whoa table and instill that reverse thrust you speak of, and we work on the whoa post. In other words, I've got that dog whoaing on command.

WHOA

"So now we enter a bird's scent cone, and I say softly and simply, "Whoa," and the dog hopefully turns to stone. We've got a pointing Lab. A Lab with a horrible pointing style, mind you, a tail at 10 o'clock, a looseness, a drooped head looking down at the bird. Let's face it, we don't have an intense English pointer on birds. We've got a good old, mellow, happy going, let's-do-it-at-our-ease, Labrador retriever. Not that some Labs aren't fired up. They are. They'll have so much vinegar in them they'll leap and slam down on a planted bird six feet away.

"So let's review. How does the average retriever go to a bird? How does this dog get steady to wing and shot? If the Labs want to point when they're young, that's fine. If they don't, I go ahead and put them on the whoa table and teach them whoa up there. You know, I stand before them like a traffic cop and tell them 'Whoa,' and should they move, I pick them up and put them back where they left. And then I put them on the whoa post. Now there are no birds involved in any of this. Not at this time at all. I don't want these dogs to associate yard work–which is negative–with birds.

"I continue this training until the dog is feeling good and standing there. Feeling good about himself again. For we had to put him down some to get this steadiness accomplished.

"Whoa is a good command for a Lab since it means something good is going to happen or is already happening. It's like the whistle.

ACROSS THE SCENT CONE

"Okay, now I work the dog on a check cord, and I like to come across the scent cone because if there's a lot of wind and you come into the scent cone, a Lab has a miracle nose and he can smell that bird quite far away. That means he's got to walk forward on scent to see the bird, and that's not good. Means the dog can crowd the bird too much and lose him. A wild bird, that is, not necessarily a tame one.

"So when the pointing retriever hits that scent cone, I just whisper whoa, no screaming at them. Just softly, whoa. Then I say, good, good. Pretty soon that dog will really start slamming into that point, as much as a retriever can, just through repetition.

"Then I have a bird boy loft the bird and fly it, or later, I work the pointing Lab on a check cord and handle the bird myself. And this is important, if the Lab moves on point or breaks point, I don't reprimand him. I don't say anything. I just pick him up and put him back where he left.

INTENSITY

"But as I say, I really don't like a pointing Lab, and here's why. When I see a dog on point, I want to see that rigid tail, those trembling flanks, that arched neck, and those expanded nostrils. I think pointers love to point. I think it's a good sensation for them. You saw my pointer, Witt, yesterday on quail. She likes to point. You could tell it. She thinks that's fun. And myself? I like to see a real stylish point, and you're not going to get that any time soon with a Lab.

Another kind of intensity. From out of the past one of the author's Labs outruns English pointer after fly-away.

"And another thing. The hunter—what do most guys do? The dog goes on point and they go berserk. They go running and screaming, 'He's got a bird, get the bird...'"

"I say relax. This is a special moment God has given us." [Don't you love Gary? He's so sensible about everything. So solid. And he extends his feelings so far beyond where we usually go. He's something special.]

He goes on to say, "This dog is intent. He's on game. So why don't you just stand there and appreciate it...enjoy it. Too many hunters don't care about that dog. All they care about is that damned bird.

"And it's so easy for the dog to break point when the hunter runs forward. To break point and rush in and flush the bird. Now you're all messed up, right?

Thirty years later, on another field, with other dogs, English pointer wins the race. As Gary prepares to loft planted bird, both dogs are pointing.

"So that's about it," says Gary, his soft voice drifting off to become softer still. "A Lab will point. But is that what you want…"

Gary's question hangs there for you to answer. I'm not sure it's a pointing Lab we need, but we could all use Gary as our dog trainer or our adviser. How blessed the guy is who can drive out to Gary's kennel when he wants and just watch him train or listen to him talk to the dogs or—best of all—just talk to him about gun dogs.

WILD BIRDS

I told you up front I'd show you the yard drills and explain how to use them, and I admonished you not to use them until you read Gary's system of whistle training. Then I further claimed a better method of training shooting retrievers was bringing them along exclusively on wild birds.

133

Gary takes bobwhite from pointing retriever. A fitting wrap-up for a do-it-all dog.

Well, let's examine this assertion, this claim that natural training before wild birds in open vistas is the best way to bring a gun dog along. I admit, you've got to have the birds and the vistas, right? And if you don't, then you're going to have to make one of those "life" decisions–whether you're going to stay in the city and make a living or move to the country so you can be a part of nature's plan and experience the glory of a bona fide shooting retriever.

I made that decision and kept to it so long as arthritis would let me stay. Many other like-minded expatriates are still out there and more joining them every day. You have to decide if you want to number among them. What it amounts to is–your life.

Training on Wild Birds

*This is the way momma-dog trained her brood
for centuries. It's the natural way to go. One hitch,
however: you've got to live where the endless fields
are available and there are lots of wild birds and
the game laws say you can train any time of the
year except when mothers-in-waiting are vulnerable
and peeps are defenseless. And my friends, it's
fascinating to realize this is exactly how gun dogs
are trained in Great Britain from whence we got
our dogs, our game, and the morals and etiquette
to take the whole shebang to the fields.*

There are several gun dog men who train only on wild birds.
Men who've never had a minute of yard drill with their gun
dogs, or at least haven't for the past 30 years.

These men are pretty much all alike: independent and self
reliant as a grizzly, legs of a Clydesdale, a snapping turtle's grasp
in their right hand from forever toting that shotgun, and a suspi-
cion of anyone who's content to live in a city. But one man who
exemplifies all the rest for me is Ben Williams of Livingston,
Montana.

Ben's a retired schoolteacher, 63 years old, who talks with a trip-
ping cadence, sports a white mustache, and has Aqua Velva eyes
from forever squinting into that endless Montana horizon.

Oh yes, Ben's a former professional assistant field trial trainer,
and I don't know what all else. I had to learn on my own that Ben
is a world class sculptor with work in major museums. What's
important to us is this: Ben has the best dogs in the world, and he
trains them only on wild birds.

135

Now, let me explain that. Usually these wild bird trainers specialize in one bird species, and they're out there day after week after month after year after year 'til death. So that one species of bird is all those dogs hunt. They become experts, the human partner is an expert. So on those treaded fields, on any given day, there's not another gun dog in the world who could equal them. They are the best, okay?

Let me explain further. Ben Williams and his pack are Hungarian partridge specialists, but they also hunt sharptail grouse and pheasant. It's just that if left to their druthers, they'd stick with the Huns.

HOW IT'S DONE

There's no sky in the big sky country the afternoon I bring you to Livingston, Montana. The distended belly of a mammoth rain cloud lays on the Toyota truck hood like an elephant udder. It drizzles, and I look off at a prairie the brilliant color of gray.

Ben tells me, "I've trained 130 dogs of my own and 170 others as a pro's assistant. Used to do all that hand signal stuff, you know, getting the dogs ready for field trials. But I've gotten completely away from that. My idea now is let the dogs go and do their own thing and they'll be better hunters for me.

"So you never have one drill," I ask, "One planted bird, one training session in the backyard?"

"Nope, never. It's not needed. Matter of fact that sort of thing can hurt a hunting dog."

I nod as I smile and ask, "Then tell me what you do to make these bird dogs of yours."

"When a Pup is six months old," says Ben, "I take him with the pack, and you must understand, I run long-legged, big-winded prairie Brittanies.

"I'm a hunter who leaves the truck in the morning and won't come back until that night. Matter of fact, hunting birds all year long is important enough to me I have two identical 4-wheel drive trucks. If one won't start, I put the dogs in the other and we take off.

"So I must have dogs who'll stay out here with me. Big-running dogs with lots of gas, high octane. Now, I've been breeding this special line of Brittanies for 30 years. Started out with field trial,

It's raining in Montana folks, as a cloud leans back to sit on the slope of a hill. Dots in foreground are hunters. The few dots in bacground are full-grown trees. This is mighty big country.

horseback Brittanies out of Pampa, Texas. Then gradually I select-bred them for exactly the job I have to do in this big prairie. You see an average size hunting area for me is 40,000 acres. That's what we're going to hunt today. Of course I have some small parcels, 3,000 acres or so, but the dogs are really bred and conditioned for larger ranches.

"Now, sometimes I'll start an exceptional pup at 3 1/2 months, depends on what the pup's showing, and I just take the young ones along with the old, seasoned ones. That's all there is to it. That'll make you the best bird hunter in the world.

"Like I say, I never show the pups a pigeon or anything. Not one yard drill. Everything is done at their leisure in the' field, always on wild birds in all kinds of weather and terrain and wind. The dogs learn all that stuff. They become experts at everything related to a Hungarian partridge in Montana.

Hunching down in the rain for photo, Ben gathers pack before him.

"Now when that pup finds out he can't catch those birds, he starts to self-break. He breaks himself. I don't have to do it.

"But one thing I demand: the dogs must back. That's because I may have a pack of six or eight dogs before me. I can't have them all trying to steal the same point."

See any similarity between what Ben's doing with his Brittanies and what Jim Culbertson and I do with our Labs? We're gang banging those birds, plus we get the bonus of training pups as we go, having the time of our lives, and the dogs are, too.

"Now, it's a mortal sin among dog men," says Ben, "to have their dogs chase a flyaway bird." To that he grins and harrumphs a, "Bosh," as he adds, "I couldn't care less...so long as they come back.

"You take Winston, one of the six smartest bird dogs I've ever had (you see how precise Ben is: he's got Winston's ranking down to an exact figure, and that's out of 300 dogs). Winston knows exactly what we're doing out there. He knows the land and the

Ben loads prairie Brittanies into mini-truck with aid of homemade ramp.

bird. Since I hunt Hungarian partridge almost exclusively, Winston certainly knows this bird. Huns fly a long way and Winston goes after them, but get this: not to chase them, but to find them again. And he does it time after time again.

"Winston can produce Huns.

"Now I do carry a whistle," Ben tells me, "but all I do with it is call the dogs to me.

"The thing is, my dogs are just free running dogs. I'm very, very strong on natural field training and letting the dog use its natural ability to hunt.

"And something else. I won't breed a dog that I had to train. For that's "me" doing the performing in that dog, get it? And he can't throw "me" in the whelping bin. So I breed only the natural dog who does it all "*without training.*" And if the dog throws true, I know what I'm going to get in that pup.

"Another way of saying it is this: I don't want to force a dog to do all these things, then think he's a great dog, then breed him thinking I'm going to get a great pup. I won't. I'll just get a mediocre dog that I would have to work on day and night to make even the slightest hunter. Understand?"

Yes, I certainly do understand. Ben speaks the ideal. I've heard it said man contributes but 5 percent to the dog's excellence in the bird field. The dog had better come from the womb with the other 95 percent, beause there's no way man can add it. You can't plant weed seeds and grow roses. The great dog's got to be in the breeding, not in the training.

Ben has kept on talking, and I've missed part of what he said, when I hear, "I'll explain what I mean by a natural trained dog. On any given day, Winston will learn the wind's at his back. So what does he do? He runs away out and turns back to me, pushing the birds to my gun."

You're going to meet Winston in a later chapter, only his breed is Lab and his name is Web. Web does the same thing on pheasant and blue grouse and chukar and all type of wild fowl for his human partner, Mike Gould, as Winston does for Ben. And yes, Web has had some yard drills, but Mike's lifelong emphasis for this dog has been wild birds and the enhancement of his natural abilities, so Web was trained on wild birds in the bird fields.

Ben's telling me, "I don't want a dog steady to wing and shot when hunting Huns. You've got to know what Huns do. When you find them, they run. And when you pin them down and shoot, they fly forever. Well, Winston knows that, so he breaks to chase them and point again. Yes, he breaks on wing and shot: he better if I want any birds. So none of my dogs are steady to wing and shot because I want to keep them in birds.

"And there's all sorts of tricks. You see most newcomers to this country will walk the shrub-clogged ditches. Not me. I walk up and down each successive rolling hill (there's those Clydesdale legs). Why? Because my dogs find the elevation the birds are feeding or loafing that day, and they hunt only at that elevation on each successive hill. So you see what I'm talking about? I'm talking about hunting dogs, not drilled dogs. I'm talking about bird dogs who know the country and the bird because that's the only place they've ever been trained.

"Now, I only missed two days hunting last year," says Ben. "I usually average about 120 days, which includes both carrying a gun and a camera (oh yes, Ben's a professional cameraman with many credits in outdoor magazines). My interest is not killing birds, it's hunting." Then he turns and asks me direct, "You know the difference?' "

I smile as I nod yes.

Ben steps from the truck, grabs a portable ramp and leans it against the kennel compartments, then opens the door of a dog box. The Brittanies pour out, ready to go. They look fit, firm, favored. Then Ben goes to the next crate door, and another wave of Brits leap to earth.

I hear Ben saying something as he's unloading the dogs, but the rain's drowning him out. I think he's told us enough, though. I said up front, the best way to train a versatile shooting retriever is on wild game in big country. Just because Ben runs Brittanies doesn't change things. A dog is a dog. Now you can see what a difference natural training makes.

Ben revealed more than one aspect of bird hunting with his natural-trained shooting dogs that should have caught your ear. It's the way to go.

FINALLY

Now at long last, we're finally ready to head where we first started to go. We're off to The Flying B Ranch outside Kamiah, Idaho. That's in the north part of the state on Lewis and Clark's return trail.

We can assure ourselves we've done our homework to get there. We've yard trained and natural trained; we learned what a pointing retriever is and how to create one; then we learned what it's like and the benefits obtained from training exclusively on wild birds.

Now we're ready to take a hand-selected bunch of four retriever trainers and the best of their progeny to field on liberated birds and see what happens when the dogs are told to self cast, to hunt on their own, to enter the bird's scent cone, present their find to the gun, and fetch the deadfall to hand.

Let's go.

Mike Gould: trainer extraordinaire, puts backward-thrust whoa into English pointer.

※

Heading for the Flying B Ranch

I'd learned what happened when you go to a kennel club to start a new gun dog organization. You watch your intentions disintegrate. So to start a new Versatile Shooting Retriever movement, I decided to call on the guys I loved and trusted. Men who thought like I did, and wanted the same thing for America's gun dogs.

There were four gun dog trainers besides myself I wanted involved in founding the Versatile Shooting Retriever movement. They are multiple breed gun dog trainer and Flying B Ranch manager, Mike Gould, Kamiah, Idaho; Butch Goodwin, Chesapeake Bay retriever training specialist, New Plymouth, Idaho; Gary Ruppel (pronounced Roopel), whistle-training puppy specialist and pointing retriever trainer, Parker, Colorado; and a new convert, Jim Charlton, golden retriever specialist, Portland, Oregon.

Plus there was the keystone in the arch of this gun dog group: Bob Burlingame, who dug a world-based business out of the dirt, owner of the Flying B Ranch, avid outdoor sportsman, and retriever lover.

HOW IT CAME ABOUT

For ten years I followed Mike Gould up and down the west slope of the rockies as he squatted and trained dogs along the Colorado River. He was opportunity's nomad and he had a rough go of it, starting with dogs hidden under his house trailer in a mobile home park that permitted no dogs. And then going with a big-buck operator who built an exquisite shooting preserve but couldn't get squared away with Mike. Then becoming independent again and leasing land to build and operate his own game preserve, plus take in gun dogs for training, and all the time I'd be showing up.

We'd run the high country, train dogs, cast a line in a mountain brook. Or since Mike was a native of this country, we'd act respectable and seek permission to fish hot spots that Mike knew about…for he'd poached them as a kid.

Then as always, Mike would prove to me that at 10,000 feet a Jeep only needs two inside tires touching dirt to circumnavigate a mountain. And we'd walk the high parks looking off at multiple mountain ranges and sitting in lush meadows watching the raptors and being embraced by the breeze, scent, and the sun.

Finally, we'd all pull into Carbondale, Colorado, at dusk and frequent the local pub, where you could get a fire-eating chili-hamburger that could cure cancer while you watched the locals play macho with the thin-walled beer cans.

And always it was the talk. Do dogs read our minds? Or do they trigger off scent? ESP, maybe that's it? Anyway you look at it, it has to be telepathic.

"Do you realize how hard the mountain spirit has to work to keep his mountain in order?" Mike would ask. "A fire sweeps through. Do you know how calamitous that is? The mountain spirit must get to work fast mending his home. Or the creeks flood out, or the beavers stop them up, or a boulder drops into the channel. The spirit's always at work, always keeping order.

"That's it," Mike would say, "order. Nature requires order and yet, did you ever notice everything in nature meanders? Continental plates wander, streams wander, trails wander. Then why must field trial Labs run a straight line for a blind plant?"

We'd talk forever and include any subject. It didn't have to make "sense" to us as it does to most people. We'd find our best breakthroughs came as we considered something others would regard as hogwash.

Well, it was that way. Mike would talk of the problems dealing with the gun dog public, with the trust-fund babies that rolled

Butch Goodwin and the love of his life, Maggie.

Gary Ruppel leaves kennel after day's work for long drive home. In his arms, Scarlet, the 8-week-old wonder, asks photographer, "Just what are you doing?"

down from Aspen with their Lab sitting in the front seat of the new Jaguar convertible. How it was always these low-rollers who wouldn't pay their training bill.

We'd train and laugh and carry on, and for those few days each summer, I was sure there was a God in heaven, I'd met his fairest child on earth, and I was blessed.

Then in the winter we'd exchange letters. Mine would be short and to the point, typed out between authoring pages in a new book. But Mike might have been put inside by deep snow or the sniffles, for his letters would continue page after page, and I would revel in their insight and simple honesty and the man's genius in walking on the bottom side of the dirt of nature, of seeing the roots of things, or of living under the whitewater of the river and feeling the heartbeat of each thing that went by. I'll give you an example.

It is January 9 as Mike writes:

"All animal species play out their respective roles in front of our eyes each day but really, who notices?

"How does a beaver instinctively know to slow down the velocity of the creek? How does he understand how to build at least eight different types of dams. Is it through watching his father and mother, his uncle or grandfather? How can he know he is responsible for initiating a process that will change a mountain creek into a series of ponds, then to a rich riparian zone, then to a meadow, then to a stable plant community, and on and on.

"As you know I've been studying game birds for quite some time now. I have told you of some of the mysteries I have witnessed. On many occasions I have seen an entire flock alert and start making an "eeeeeeee" sound, a soft sound but at the same time, chilling to me. Each bird in the flock, no matter if there is 20 or 200 is standing alert and holding completely still, no dusting or running or feeding or drinking, completely still.

"I have learned to slowly scan the sky while the birds are in this state and always a raptor will appear within a minute or so. [Dogs also know things before they happen. Mike and I talk of this a lot.] The predator was not visible when the birds alerted, they could not have seen him prior to their display. After the raptor flies past, the flock goes back to their normal routine without a glance in his direction. How do they know he is coming? They don't alert to a heron or a magpie or a stellar jay. How do they know the difference between a predator and a meadow lark a full minute before they can see it? "The U.S. Forest Service," continues Mike, "claims a forest will harvest itself by means of a fire event about every 40 to 60 years. I often wonder how the forest prepares itself before the fire. What animals are involved and what roles do they play. [See the circle of cause and effect Mike interprets in nature?] For sure the porcupine plays an active role by helping to supply fuel. Dry summer weather and some insects help to relieve a forest of it's moisture. When the fire starts, the

147

Jim Charlton, the golden specialist, sits on bow of boat with Sage, possibly the best golden water dog I've ever seen.

winds rally it into a frenzy and from there the fire creates it's own wind and momentum.

"Bill, you and I have discussed the theory of the ripple that people send through the natural environment when they enter into it. How could we be so ignorant to assume we could hunt, hike, fish, trap, or drive a gasoline-powered vehicle into the natural world without being detected? We are the only species with the ability to destroy the earth and we are almost totally unaware of the natural controls within it.

148

"Do you believe it's possible that we have overlooked our god-given guide to the natural world? Isn't it absurd to think of the treatment the dogs have endured for so long–and Bill, you care so much about this–when they very well could be our equal.

"My goals concerning breeding and training bird dogs are very basic. I am in it for the education, not to teach. I'm too busy trying to learn from the dogs to electrically shock them into submission. I'm going to keep my eyes open while I'm out there and my sincere hope is that someday I will be accepted. I have no desire to dominate or intimidate. I desire friendship and honesty and love. I've never seen anything that could equal a dog, and I don't believe anyone else has either."

REASON FOR THIS PARTICULAR LETTER

I didn't choose this letter at random. There was a purpose in my selection. Mike writes something in there that is very important to me right now and is pertinent to you.

He wrote, "…I hope that someday I will be accepted."

Now, I'm a Ben Lilly chronicler. Ben was the world's most rough-out hunter and spent his last days in the San Juan Wilderness area northeast of Silver City, New Mexico, harvesting cattle-killing grizzlies and cougar.

Ben would enter the wilderness with his Bible, stakeout chains for his hounds, scrimshawed knife (he made himself), rifle, a sack of corn meal, some cinnamon candy in case he met a child, and that was it, nothing more, and he could stay forever. Oh, he might have to stop by an outpost or line shack or backwoods cabin to find something to nail onto his boots for soles, but other than that he was self-sufficient.

He'd kill a bear on a cold afternoon, and he'd dig out the entrails and crawl inside to sleep warm. That was where he was, inside a sow, when her boyfriend came calling one night. Ben killed the suitor, as well.

Or he'd light a dead log on fire, drag out the coals and crawl into the pit. His rag-tag clothes caught fire more than once.

One day a reporter showed up and asked Ben if he could accompany him on a hunt. Ben decidedly didn't take to the notion, and he told the reporter something the man didn't understand. But Mike and I do.

He told him, "If you are not a member of the family, you wouldn't know what you were seeing."

What Ben meant was this: if the reporter were not a member of the family of animals, he wouldn't understand anything he saw take place.

That's what I have found and shared with Mike. We understand the family of dogs, or at least we try hard to do so. We approach them at an entirely different level with a totally different mindset than most dog trainers. We give dogs credit that other trainers scoff at.

Okay, there's more.

As I'd spend those summers with Mike, we would not be alone. Mike always had his hanger's on. Specifically, Butch Goodwin, who at that time was manager of a sporting goods store, amateur Chesapeake Bay retriever trainer, and field trial aficionado. Butch would always be close by, for Mike had the finest training facilities I've ever seen. Plus, Butch was not in opposition to what Mike and I were saying, he just didn't know. So he kept frying those dogs out there with his electric shock collar, and Mike and I would grieve for his dogs–and for him.

But there are so many good things about Butch. He's the salt of the earth; he means well, and he does well. He's kind of a Salvation Army short order cook–he sincerely cares about your well being, what you're doing, and how well you're doing it.

Also, Butch is about 300 pounds, 6'4", and a former line backer for the University of Arizona Wildcats. Who's going to jump him? Not with his thrust. You see, Butch doesn't do anything gentle. Everything's gripped tight and hyped up and rammed through. Matter of fact, he can get on such a high plain of intensity that one time his university football coach called Butch to the sidelines and told him to cool it, that his incitement to destroy the opposing team was frightening his own linemen.

One time on a bear hunt, I was stoved up with arthritis but still wanted to get down the canyon wall to photograph the bear high in a tree. Never mind. Butch became, for me, a moving ponderosa. I just grabbed his belt and we went straight down, and then back up. That's Butch: the power of a human escalator. Now, there's much about Butch you're going to learn (matter of fact, he becomes very important in this book), and there's much you're going to admire before you finish this book. But this is how I met him—out there electrically sizzling those dogs—and that's how you're meeting him. But that was Saul of the Bible persecuting the Christians. Remember? Remember how Saul became Paul the pillar of the Christian church through divine intervention. Hum? Could it be?

Now we'll move on to Gray Ruppel.

You know Gary quite well by now. He was always at Mike's. Gary loves Mike, as do all of us who'd gather along the Colorado River each summer. So whenever I'd visit Mike, I'd visit Gary, first as a kennel manager, then as an apprentice trainer, and finally as a select pro with his own training kennels and a brilliant future before him. But as contributory as these guys are to my life and to my growth as a bird dog philosopher, just knowing them wouldn't have seen the birth of the Versatile Shooting Retriever movement. That took Bob Burlingame.

I don't know Bob well, he seems distant. He's a huge man, with a built-in scowl that's deceiving, because I think Bob is all heart. I think that rough exterior he wears is the shaggy bark of a cottonwood tree that hopes you don't scratch through and see the sap of the heart's kindness ooze down the trunk.

A former Navy fighter pilot and a crackerjack, present-day business flyer, Bob recently put his twin-turbo prop Commander in a mud field next to a forest ranger station and had to scrounge wood planks to take off again. He'd been told the land was for sale and wondered how it would fit into the Flying B's hunting plans.

I don't know much more about Bob, except he's kind, quick to reach for his wallet, a stellar host, and a man who will bankroll most things for wilderness, wildness, and gun dogs.

You ought to book into his hunting lodge. He might be there. Either way, you'll have a great hunt and a great stay. The place is five-star.

And that's the point. I asked Mike if Bob would let us use his facilities, and Bob literally handed me the keys.

So Bob let me invite the people I wanted present to enjoy the luxurious rooms, our own private kitchen and cooks, great housekeeping, six gun dog assistants to help with training, land, and liberated birds, a fishing guide, a documentary TV cameraman, and on and on.

151

But that was not the end of it—as I make my way about the nation calling on gun dog notables, I'm always looking for new converts to the Tarrant stable of no-stress, no-impact gun dog trainers. And that's how I found Jim Charlton of Charlton Kennels, located on Charlton road, Sauvie Island, Portland, Oregon.

At 6'6" he's about a foot taller than I am, and when I pulled into his drive and climbed out with him standing there, I talked to his belt buckle for five minutes. But I was always at ease, for the man has a pillow voice, a loose stance, a ready smile, and a need to thank God for everything happening.

He was my kind of man.

Staying the day, I quickly took to Jim and what he stands for with dogs. And on that spot, during that day, and unbeknownst to him, I decided to invite him to the Flying B. So that made up the Flying B humane-training seminar and VSR workshop.

And why was Bob Burlingame staking all this, why was I promoting all this, and why were Mike, Butch, Gary and Jim supporting all this? Well, there are many answers. You have learned most of them by reading this far in this book. But primarily, it goes back to the introduction, where I stated that my interest in the hunting retriever movement was to keep the dogs from being hurt, that Omar Driskill wanted a way to test bona fide hunting retrievers and award them for their excellence, and that Bob Rathe, you'll recall, wanted a test format where he could keep his dogs tuned up, in training and perpetually testing them as journeyman gun dogs.

Well, all this applies here, but there's more. There's the hope that we can lift the shooting retriever public above the, "get the bird Buck." Right now, too many of us are using the retriever. That's fine. That's what he's for. But at the same time we ought to be enjoying the retriever and letting him know in our treatment, our hunting, and our training how much we admire and love him. Let him know how much he contributes to the outing and to our sense of well being, and when he's really needed, all others having forsaken us, how good a friend he is above all others.

All this was riveted into place by a letter I got from Butch Goodwin as he accepted my invitation to be present at The Flying B. Read of this man's life—in his own words—and the transition that took place in his relationship with his dogs and his view of them, his treatment of them, his love of them, his goals for them, and his dependency on them. This is what we can only hope will happen to all retriever trainers. And hope as well the seminar and workshop at the Flying B will help start the movement to bring it all to pass.

Here are the words of "Paul."

"I was one of the baby boomers, born near mid-century (1946 to be exact) in the suburbs of Washington, D.C.

"I was lucky enough to have been raised hunting Canada geese and ducks on the Chesapeake Bay in the days immediately before the bay became a mecca for commercial hunting operations. Those were the days when you could knock on a farmer's door and get permission to hunt on his place. Those were the days before you had to be a powerful "Beltway insider," or a wealthy contributor to get invited to hunt on one of the many extensive private hunting leases. Those were the last of the glory days of Chesapeake Bay waterfowl gunning.

"I have my first memories of the impressive Chesapeake Bay retrievers found along the eastern shore of the Bay during this time. I believe that this is what spurred my interest in this great breed of retrievers.

"College took me to the desert at Tucson, Arizona, with limited waterfowl hunting, but lots of time to hunt quail and coyotes. While I was studying commercial art and learning that there was a big step from the sport of high school football to the business of college football, my father was suddenly stricken with numerous and frequent heart attacks. Within a matter of months he had passed away, and I found myself without my lifelong "leader by example." This was a tough time.

"As the years passed and a marriage came and went, I found myself living in the mountains of Colorado, traveling as a sales rep for a sporting goods wholesaler peddling guns and fishing tackle and having the opportunity to hunt waterfowl and big game all over the west. I began to travel with a dog crate in the back of my company car and when I stopped at night, I found myself making sure it was a good area where I could train my dog.

"I got serious about having a well-trained retriever because my hunting partners always had dogs that were untrained, always out of control, and losing many of the birds that we shot. Training my

Chesapeakes helped me through the tough times of a divorce and gave me a new direction and focus for my life: definitely for the better. Suddenly a whole new world opened up and became a much better place. I feel that I owe one Chessie named Bomber (and some other friends who I'll mention later) a lot. They made all of the difference. And whether they were dog or human, I heard what they had to say. Even though sometimes I didn't heed what I heard.

"I think I was very lucky when I decided to get serious about training retrievers. I knew that I wanted to have a good Chesapeake, I was impressed with their stamina and toughness from my early experience on the bay. This wasn't a macho thing with me as I find it is with so many hunters. I just wanted a dog that I felt could handle the hardship of hunting the Colorado River with its big ice flows in the minus-10 degree weather that was common during goose season.

"I happened to fall into an extremely well-bred Chesapeake who I rescued from a life of being chained to a tree. Bomber was almost a year old when I borrowed a friend's Blazer to drive the 90 miles it took to look at him. Chained to a tree at the side yard, I was told that he would fetch the biggest stick that you could throw for him.

"I knew little about Chesapeake breeding, but Bomber came home with me and spent 11 of his next 15 years retrieving ducks and geese instead of sticks. Bomber and I hunted most of the United States; all the way from the Colorado River to the Chesapeake Bay.

"When I did learn something about Chesapeake breeding it came to pass Bomber was the son of FC-AFC-CFC-CAFC Chesdel Chippewa Chief (the only Chesapeake to ever hold both Canadian and American FC and AFC titles) and a grandson of Dual Ch Capital City Jake on his mother's side (one of only 12 dual champions in Chesapeake breed history). *[Editors note: a dual champion is a dog who wins championships in both field trials and on the show bench.]*

"A short time after acquiring Bomber, I was fortunate to meet someone else who has had a profound influence on my life: Mike Gould. Mike always stuck by his beliefs in the importance of gun dogs at a time when I was being snookered into the field trial-, and later test hunt-game.

154

"Mike was an exceptional and innovative trainer and teacher who was free with his advice (whether I wanted and listened to it or not), and he extended unlimited use of his facilities to me so I could train dogs. Through the years Mike and I have clashed on several occasions, but I have never lost my respect nor admiration for him and his convictions. He's a good friend and has taught me a lot.

"Mike began our friendship by teaching me everything that he could about training retrievers. He could see that my interest was being "pulled" by outside influences toward competing in field trials and the newly conceived hunt tests. And Mike was very critical of my interest in a high pressure, electric collar, training program.

"Little did either of us know that in my thirst for learning all that I could about training retrievers, I would eventually come full circle and realize that I should have not only heard what Mike was telling me, but listened to what he was saying, as well. Like most of the dog game crowd, my tremendous competitiveness and hunger for self-gratification grew virtually unchecked.

"If I owe Mike Gould my respect and appreciation, I owe Maggie even more, for she was the dog that bore the brunt of my training mistakes. Maggie taught me how to train retrievers. She and I learned about everything that it takes to make a well-trained, high-pressure, collar-trained retriever and we learned it together, as a team. But what we didn't learn was how to have fun as a team. I thought I was having fun, but I can only now imagine Maggie's feelings.

"As my knowledge, interest, and love for the Chesapeake breed grew, I labored over the possibility of breeding my outstanding dog. I knew that, although Maggie was exceptional, I had to try to improve on what I had. I bred Maggie to an outstanding young dog with all of the quality that you could ever want in a Chesapeake. At my request, Mike stepped in and chose a fine male pup with tremendous conformation and exceptional natural ability for me from the litter.

"Soon after this, Linda Harger, a nationally recognized leader in professional Chesapeake Bay retriever trainers, came through Colorado on her way to the Chesapeake Specialty Field Trial and stopped to train with me. This started the ball rolling for me to move to Idaho and work for Linda at her North Star kennel and a a chance to be involved with some of the finest Chesapeakes in the country. My dedication to the Chesapeake was significantly increased by this experience.

"Like many of life's experiences, often you don't see the significance of what you're doing until after it's over. The experience of working for a field trial pro precipitated a change and rethinking of my priorities. I suddenly came to the realization that most of the field trial retrievers were much better at performing in competition but had little or no natural hunting instinct. So often, it soon became evident, a lot of additional training was necessary to turn a field trial dog into a good hunting companion. Most field trialers don't want their dogs to use their natural instincts as it is contrary to the game that they play.

"Now why did I become involved with the Chessies in the beginning? Because I wanted a well-trained retriever that I could take hunting. It didn't take me long to realize that the AKC licensed field trials had gone completely off the deep end in their testing procedures and the training pressure necessary to run in these events had to follow in order to stay competitive. The field trial game had gotten out of hand. The training had become very sophisticated because it had to match the game. The game had to, therefore, become more sophisticated because of the advanced training. It became a vicious circle. And the dogs were the ones who were paying the price.

"I began to realize that the only hope for the salvation for the retriever breeds was the non-competitive test hunts. The hunting retriever clubs presented a great opportunity to avail almost anyone with a retriever the chance to test their dogs against a predetermined standard when they adopted the idea of the hunt test.

"When these organizations instituted their hunt test programs in the early '80s, it allowed the weekend trainer and the guy with a great gun dog the opportunity to evaluate their retriever's performance. There was now a chance to honor these proven hunting champions which the field trial game didn't afford.

"I was growing continually more disillusioned at some of the things I saw happening to retrievers in the name of training. I saw many fine animals that had great desire, and tracking instincts, and the ability to use their nose for searching—all that taken away because of the forced domination created by the electric collar.

156

"I saw trainers force their dogs to run out of fear, all the while creating the false illusion of desire. The electric collar is a very sophisticated and powerful training tool. It is a training tool which, like guns, is very easy to misuse and therefore can be much maligned. If you believe that guns don't kill people, people kill people, then it is easy to adopt the same philosophy about the collar.

"The electric collar is not the problem. It is a tool that needs to be used correctly. The problem is the way that it is used. The problem is the traditional high-pressure training program which still predominates in field trial training.

"A collar does not have to be brutal. It is not necessary to dominate the dog and force him into submission in order to train him. Nor is it necessary to break the dog's spirit in order to train him. It is absolutely essential that to turn out a stylish, confident retriever that the dog be trained by lots of patient teaching and repetition, and not by brutality and domination.

"I need to mention that Linda Harger is not a particularly heavy-handed trainer. I wouldn't have worked for her if she was. Most of the Chesapeakes that she trained at that time and currently, aren't even collar-trained dogs. Linda was not the problem for me, it was many of the amateurs and pros other than Linda who trained with us. Many of them had the attitude that I'm going to "…teach that SOB a lesson." And at that I became very disgusted.

When Linda quit, I had just bought a farm in western Idaho and began training gun dogs on my own. I continued to believe that the hunt tests were the retriever's salvation and because I only had AKC events in my area, I ran my dog in every AKC test hunt within traveling distance.

"I put an AKC Master Hunter title on Maggie's son, Boo, and numerous Junior and Senior titles on my young Chesapeakes. Boo and I were invited to, and participated in, the Master National Hunt Test in Minden, Nevada, and I became very disillusioned over the misrepresentation of this event as a hunt test. Why? Because it wasn't a test, and it had nothing to do with hunting. As always seems to happen, the retriever testing organizations to various degrees, caved-in to the field trial "wanna-be" crowd, and as a result we have judges who, rather than setting up hunting tests, set up watered-down field trial tests which are solely designed to trick the dogs. I would like for you to read something, Bill, that I wrote soon after I returned from the Master Nationals.

"It is nearly 4:00 a.m. and I lie awake in a motel room far from home. The television is casting eerie images over the darkened room. I take the foggy opportunity of sleeplessness to reflect on what has brought me to this place.

"On the television a young lady is selling her scheme for taking charge of your life and controlling your eating habits with the slogan, "Stop the insanity." In my semi-conscious state I have no idea what I'm watching and don't really care. I just want the TV off. The huckstering woman is loud and irritating. I fumble in the darkness for the remote changer.

"With the TV off, I can hear sounds of other test-hunt participants talking and moving around in the next room, mixed with the muffle of an occasional dog bark. Suddenly I believe I'm awake and realize that the irritating woman on the now-silent TV may well have had more of a message than I was ready to understand. I was sure that sleep wouldn't come until I put her message out of my mind. At the same time, the two Chesapeakes, mother and son, lying sprawled on the floor of the motel and now shifting to more comfortable positions put my uneasy insomnia into proper perspective.

"I came to the realization the women contestants in the next room were packing their truck for their trip back to California. I hear their mute conversation and the clatter of necessary gear being place in its exact position, and dogs being fed, watered, and loaded. I realize what has brought this group of Chesapeake Bay retriever enthusiasts to this place in the Nevada desert is exactly what is now tearing the group apart.

"I wonder what all they and their dogs had to endure to get here. I wonder if they are at all happy that they came. I doubt it. *Stop the insanity*–those words keep ringing in my mind. I stare at the ceiling and can't sleep.

"Now my mind wanders to a cold Colorado morning more than ten years before. High in the mountains on a fabled trout stream the ducks are plentiful. The greenheads strafe the ice-covered decoys glistening in the early morning sunlight. Rarely will the big birds land close to shore.

"The ducks were so smart they landed in the center of the stream or across toward the other bank, and if sufficiently relieved of all concern, would only then swim toward my decoys.

"Some goldeneyes were not so smart. They would be scudding past and suddenly see my decoys and throw themselves in. I rarely shot at these diving ducks: they taste like fish. So I allowed them to set in and dive about my decoys and add reality to my rig. But it was these goldeneyes that would later cause me a problem.

"Out of the corner of my eye I catch the streak of two dive-bombing mallards swinging past to take a look. I sense they'll give me another pass, so I swing the old hump-backed Browning and as they go by I slap the trigger. I feel the barrel recoiling into the action. It's a familiar feeling and sound since I hunt nearly every morning, but not usually in this particular spot in the river where the water is so swift on the other side. Again I fire and notice the first duck I shot gliding toward the other side of the river with his wings set. He tumbles into a field. The second duck evades my shot and flies away unscathed. But the goldeneyes–the goldeneyes which have settled in my decoy spread for nearly fifteen minutes, they explode in a cacophony of startled wing beats.

"The Chesapeake is not moving, but sitting steady, frosted with ice and watching the escaping mass of goldeneyes. He has not seen the only duck killed tumble across the river. And this dog has never been taught blind retrieves. Several attempts at throwing rocks across the river to get him to the other side end in failure.

"I have a 14-month-old Chesapeake pup at home that has been learning to run blind retrieves and he could probably do this, but it's five miles to home. I have no choice: I don't want to lose a duck. I pick up the decoys, heel the dog, and head for the truck.

"Forty minutes later and nearly two hours after I had shot the mallard, I line up my young hopeful and point her straight across the river. At the command, "Back," she shoots into the water and swims hard as she confronts the current and floating ice on the far side.

The river current carries her down stream about fifty yards. The chunks of ice battering her. She reaches the other side thinking she's kept a correct line and continues up the far hill. I stop her with a single blast on the whistle and give her a left-hand cast to move her back upstream, to put her in a straight line to where the bird actually went in.

Another stop and a back cast sends her into the field where I had last seen the duck. She disappears from sight. And I hoarsely yell after her, "…hunt 'em up," as I keep my frozen fingers crossed.

"Awakening from my recollection, consciousness brings the realization that my neighbors have started their truck and are heading off into the darkness. The two dogs stir and one looks out the motel window as they drive off, but settles back on the floor as things calm down. I realize they are among the first to leave. After several days of casual conversations, they left without so much as a word. I am sure they too, are not happy.

"I lay there in the dark and take stock of what it took to get here, and wondered, then, where do we go now? I realize that everyone who had qualified and came to this National test for Master Hunter dogs had been through the same thousands of hours of training and thousands of miles of traveling.

"For what? A test that was not what it was billed to be. We were supposed to have attended and competed in a national gun dog test. But what we were presented had nothing to do with a true hunting situation. And that's what the rules required. And now the majority of us had been eliminated from running by the tricks of judges who should have kept judging their classic field trials and stayed away from this master national.

"My thoughts turned to the dogs who had endured those thousands of hours of training, some of it very brutal I'm sure, in order to get to this event. And they were swept away like a slap in the the face and never tested for gun dogs, in the doing of it.

"I could see why the girls in the next room wanted to go home. Who needs this? My priorities had changed.

"'*Stop the insanity.*' Now it was all beginning to come together. Much of the training which these fine animals were required to endure in order to get to this point was truly insanity. For what? A ribbon? A silver plate? All for the owner!

"My thoughts returned to the young Chesapeake running the blind retrieve across the icy river to try to fetch a mallard shot several hours before. She tried that day with more heart than most people muster in a lifetime. And, here she was, now crippled from tick-caused arthritis (Lyme disease) and so retired. Lying on the

160

motel floor next to her son who only hours before had shown the same kind of heart and intelligence. And because of that, had been tricked out of–what was supposed to be–the biggest event in which he had participated. I decided to go home and take him hunting. That was real.

"Searching for sleep in the now quiet motel room, I see in my mind's eye the young Chesapeake show up as a brown blur upstream from where I had cast her for the duck. She was carrying the still-alive mallard as she entered the harsh current and swam toward me. All of it just as we had done hundreds of hours in training.

"These are the real champions, I thought. Who needs an audience?

"That duck will hang forever on my living room wall. It so overshadows the ribbons that hang in my office that I no longer need, nor want. They were not for the real thing."

Signed: Butch Goodwin, Western Idaho, November 1994

Then Butch offers this addendum:

He writes, "You know I can't help but think of the words of one of the great retriever men, Charley Morgan, when he said, '…his happiest clients were those whose dog would get a duck out of the back pond. While the unhappiest clients were those whose dog hadn't won the national.' It's sad when keeping score becomes more important than doing the real thing.

"I spent a lot of time sitting in a duck blind this past season thinking about where I was in my training and breeding and where I wanted to go with my program. Although I don't believe there is such a thing as an all-purpose dog as you hope we can achieve Bill, I do believe we should be trying our best to produce a multi-purpose dog.

"I have, therefore, changed my entire mind set and my entire training program."

IN GRATITUDE

No way could this book and all it stands for have received a more critical and appropriate testimonial. Butch "Paul" Goodwin has stated the total case before us, and as a born-again, no-stress trainer, has shown us the way to follow.

This is not to say our regard is any less for the other partici- pants at this seminar and workshop. Every man who owns a retriever must be indebted, and in gratitude, to each trainer here for what they've done, and are doing, in creating a better shooting companion for each of us.

The retriever will never be the same again. He will be more than any of us ever imagined. But he will be no more than what God intended when He made him.

Now, on with the Flying B versatile shooting retriever project.

❋

The Running

The French have a term, 'Laissez faire,' which means the practice of letting people act without interference. I feel that's how gun dogs are best trained and hunted.

Heat comes to northern Idaho early this spring. The temperature registers in the 80s and it is humid. Way too hot for good dog work.

Though miles of land are owned or leased by the Flying B Ranch, still it makes everything easier if we run the dogs adjacent to the huge flight pens.

We're out there in Timothy and pepper grass, with a field of yellow-crowned rape off to the east (rape, or canola: a plant raised for its low saturated fats; the seed produces an oil used in salad dressings). The land rolls away in soft undulations toward the south, while the same scene appears to the west, and both flight pens and farm improvements short-stop everything heading north.

The sky is cloudless on this May day, bright with a searing sun, and void of breeze. That pepper grass is so pungent with odor it is stifling. The whole field seems to be draining chlorophyll, buckets and buckets of suffocating chlorophyll.

There are complaints from some present, but I figure it's real life, when is everything perfect in the fall, when you're actually hunting for birds?

Bob Burlingame and Mike Gould have saved us scads of pheasants and bobwhite. Although the birds are in molt, the pheasants still sport long tails and luminous plumage.

Putting off enough odor for the retrievers to smell, however, is a different matter for these birds. Had nature already descented them for this helpless period of their year, or was it the pungency of chlorophyll that just drowned everything else out?

WORKSHOP

We start the workshop. Bird boys plant the pheasant hard, which means the birds are spun mightily, head tucked under a wing, and that wing placed to earth. To help keep the bird motionless, they are also stretched–that is, the legs are pulled straight down and the body held taut, which seems to make some birds comatose.

CLEAN EARTH

It is our intention to run each dog on clean earth, so we start to the far east and work to the west, moving about 10 yards each time for the subsequent bird plant. This means coming down a pitch of about four degrees.

THE MIND SET

There are four trainers participating. Jim Charlton brings two goldens: Sage who is a 6½-year-old male and Paige, a 3-year-old female. Jim is a traditional trainer. He's been at it 30 years and knows what he's doing.

Butch Goodwin has Maggie, the 11½-year-old love of his life, who is getting by on steroids since she suffers from arthritis brought about by a 3½-year siege with Lyme disease. Also wearing Butch's colors is Maggie's son, Boo. Butch is another traditionalist who is starting to incorporate bits and pieces of the *laissez faire* gang.

Mike Gould fields 10-month-old Camas (Camas being an edible root favored by the Nez Perce), a totally naturally trained female pup (and daughter of Web), who has done nothing during her short life except hunt wild birds and has never had one yard drill. Backing her up is 10-year-old Web, the miracle Lab, who could best any retriever in America in any bird field on any day, and Rudy, an 8-month-old male wonder, also a pup from Web. Mike believes the less control for a dog is the best.

164

Gary Ruppel is present with whistle-trained Scarlet. Remember Scarlet? Just seeing her move prompts larceny. You want to snatch her up and run to the hills where the two of you will never be found. Scarlet's now 4 months old and hasn't a second to rest. With her is Witt, Gary's English pointer, and Kodak, a 6-year-old Lab. Also in Gary's dog crates are 2-year-old Annie, a yellow pointing Lab, and another pointing Lab, this one black, who is 2-year-old Zeb. Gary's training program is built around maximum freedom for the dog.

WHERE I DIRECTED MY ATTENTION

Before any of us arrived at the Flying B, before I even sent out invitations, I predicted how the four handlers would approach the shooting retriever workshop. Gary and Mike have worked on the principles supporting the VSR for years, but Jim Charlton is the newcomer, and he's naturally been raised and tutored by a traditional school. That's the way he trains: with sufficient control of the dog to always have prompt response to a command.

As for Butch, well, Butch being a born-again trainer doesn't mean he's attained total redemption. This Mac truck of a man has spent his entire dog career living the imperative that he be in charge. To let a dog have his head in the field is beyond his capability. I happen to know Butch will one day achieve just that, but he isn't there yet.

So we have two handlers with *total confidence in their dogs*, and we have two handlers with total *confidence in their control.* Nothing is ever that clear-cut, but the characterizations are generally true.

The first two handlers listed above have let their dogs self-train, with ultimate latitude, achieving maximum confidence. The latter two have taken their dogs through yard drills and basic obedience and only later did they let them run in the fields. Even at field, these men's dogs are under control at all times. The dogs of these latter two men have confidence all right, but it is not in themselves. Instead, it is in the trusworthiness of the handlers.

Now, I do not paint Jim Charlton with the traditional field trial brush I seem to describe above. Jim is a soft man, a thoughtful man, a kind man. At all times he's going to do what's best for his dogs. But I repeat, Jim has received and excelled with traditional training.

That's not what Mike, Gary and I are about. We are about nontraditional training. So we do not, as Ben Williams of Livingston, Montana, says, "Teach dogs anything we don't have to." Okay?

DON'T LET THIS GET BY YOU

Now, what I'm writing here is vitally important, for these are the stages you, the reader, will go through if you intend to develop a VSR and have previously handled field trial prospects. It'll take you some time to let go, to let the dog have his prerogative, to let the dog's natural abilities emerge without you shaping them in your own image.

It's like handing your 16-year-old the keys to your car. Have you trained him well enough? Do you trust him enough? Will he break? Will he bolt? Will he self destruct?

TWO TYPES OF RETRIEVERS

Mike and Gary believe (and I know it's a fact) that the pup given his head from the litter box on will never let you down. He'll always self correct, he'll always figure his way out of a predicament, and he'll always contribute more to any outing than a rigidly dominated dog trained with a heavy hand.

For the limited dog, the dog that's always been kept in fetters, within invisible rails, within voice command and whip command, and never beyond the shout of threats, this dog cannot function on his own. Let him disappear from his handler's sight and he crumbles; he panics. He figures he has no one to lead him, and without a leader, he's been convinced he's helpless.

He further knows if he goes back to find his handler, he may be punished. This is a very unhappy dog; a dog with a bleeding ulcer; a dog who bites his nails.

But what's the disposition of the do-it-all dog? Well, he has no time to fret. There's always another clump to crash, hill to climb, stream to swim, and scent to ponder. If he wants a different happiness than he finds in the field, then all he must do is look for his human partner who'll rub his ears, massage his tummy, and tell him in joyful voice he's the greatest thing that ever lived. As any one could predict, this is a happy pup. He'll never be on Prozac.

We did not go to the Flying B Ranch to find a winner but to work retrievers as shooting dogs. That is, to prove that deep down in every retriever there is a natural, versatile performer. Every dog present worked game into the bag as well as shown here. Web, Mike's miracle dog, points (or delay whoas) pheasant.

So What Happens?

With the heat of the day, the pungency of the cover, and the lack of breeze, the dogs couldn't find the planted birds. They self cast, ran a beat, converted that to a sweep, went in circles, overlapped, and finally hesitated to scratch their heads. I watched superlative shooting dogs pass within three feet of a planted bird and not alert on its scent. I also watched many birds stand and

167

Pheasant volunteers and leaps to wing.

run away. Sometimes, the bird would regain his senses and just launch to flight.

Some of the handlers cried foul ball. But that's an old field trialer's cry.

With each live bird we planted, a dead bird was placed some 20 yards distant on the same line, the theory being if by some fluke the dog missed the live bird, he might stumble onto the dead one. To no avail—the bird work was pathetic.

Mike Gould approached me and said, "It's molt and these birds don't trust themselves to fly. So as soon as they revive from the plant, they're taking off running. That's why we can't find them.

In a blur, this big exotic bird beats for life.

The dog should trail, sure, but this stuff stinks so I wonder if the dog can smell anything?"

I accept Mike's analysis, but the workshop continues. Dog after dog self-casts to the bird field. Finally, yes finally, two dogs, back-to-back work the bird perfect, raise it to the gun and bring it dead to hand. Hooray!

And what two dogs are these? Web, the 10-year-old wonder that has made Mike a nationally recognized trainer, and (you'll never believe it) Butch's Maggie, the 11½-year-old Chessie. Maggie blew our mind. No one could believe her. She mince-footed to field—after all she's sick. Then she took her time making

Mike shoots bird and Web fetches.

game. Finally, entering the bird's scent cone, she walked up to stare directly down at the bird, and pointed with one front paw raised until Butch kicked the bird to flight and shot it.

I shouted in gleeful garble, "She's pointing Butch…she's pointing."

"Yea I know," he answered in muffled voice.

"Did you know she could point?" I yell. I'm really enthused.

"She pointed for me 4½ years ago down at Mike's," I'm told.

"Well, it's beautiful," I say, my surprise subsiding now. "Just beautiful." And though the gallery is applauding, it is also time for them to hush, for two retrievers, both gray muzzled, have presented the testy bird to wing and shot.

With no wind, bad cover, stink, molt, whatever, the two senior citizens have proven a man can eat supper by following a VSR. And what of these two elders? One has been big-time pressure trained with an electric collar about her neck. In other words, train-with-pain, total domination, no latitude granted.

170

Web delivers to hand, and every hunter reading this book would like to see himself in this picture with his own miracle dog.

The other has lived the life of a Mississippi kite, let's say. He flies where he wants, lands where he pleases, lifts to the wind of his preference, and just generally has a ball of a time being what God intended when he invented him, and man has not put asunder.

DOGS READ OUR MINDS

But that's not really the point. We must go back to the handlers. You know, dogs read our minds. I even wrote a book about it, *The Magic of Dogs.* So we won't go into that here.

But Maggie senses the new regard Butch has for her and for all dogs now. She knows his penchant for kindness, his raising the level of a dog's worth, and the value he now places in a dog's love. He's beginning to grant that a dog is a miracle, that a dog is best followed, not lead.

So, realizing these things, Maggie is also reborn. Maggie knows what Butch wants when he casts her to field and she hopes to please him. Thus, she pointed a pheasant out of gratitude. It's beautiful.

Which means the two dogs who performed so well were both being handled by men of the same bent. One man's approach to dogs stemming from the cradle, the other man just coming of age.

THE REST OF THE ENTRIES

Not a retriever ran that morning who would not take you upland game hunting and fill your bag. Matter of fact, I didn't see a dog afield that any avid upland bird hunter wouldn't have reached for his wallet to make a deal.

Hardly any of them missed working the bird, but the birds came out erratic. One flew directly at the camera crew and everyone had to duck. Another one, this one put up by Gary's yellow Labrador, exited so low that to shoot would have been to hazard Annie.

Then there were the running birds. Mike's Camas took after one and ran 80 yards to the left, then back toward the gallery. The bird was continually lofted out of range and Mike would shoot but his gun couldn't reach that far. Camas, the wild Indian, never gave up. She chased that bird until it flew into the flight pen from whence it had been released. Jim Charlton turned in great work with Sage. Matter of fact, on their last run they posted a perfect find and fetch.

Kodak, Gary's nonpointing Lab, chased a pheasant to the rape field and wouldn't exit. He finally came out to collapse. He'd used up so much of himself in that tall cover, with no wind and the hot sun. A fast motorcade to the horse tank and the gritty dog was dunked and revived.

Annie busted Gary's buttons when she pointed, and Gary walked to the right-hand side of her, having made an arc about the dog. Then 2½ yards to front, I can hear him whispering, whoa, whoa, whoa, as he kicks out the bird, the first handler to do

172

You can see Gary Ruppel laughing as baby Scarlet lifts B-29 bird (in proportion to her size) to wing.

so. Shooting the bird quickly, Gary received a first-class retrieve. Annie, the yellow Lab, had worked perfectly.

Mike's young pup Rudy was influence-handled into the pheasant's scent cone—after he glad handed the gallery and said hello to everyone there. Finally, Rudy saw the pheasant, jumped it, and Mike dropped it.

APPROACH

When it was all over, no shooting retriever flushed like a springer would. All came to the bird in a hesitation whoa or a look-down point. No dogs shrapnelled the birds the way Jim Culbertson's and my retrievers do. But then Jim does not shoot the first bird with his 30" barrel, 12-gauge, full-choke Model 12, until it's 40 yards out. Jim's last kill comes at 80 yards.

Also, Jim is in shape and can keep up with the pack. He has no need for a delayed whoa or a point. Me, I just accompany Jim for ballast. I shoot a featherweight, auto, 20-gauge Franchi and try to get my work done during the initial covey rise. Pecos, my 4-year-

Pheasants were prone to run before the dog, and when the dog got too near, they flew. Here, one of Mike's young male prospects has the bird take shot and scatter feather just in front of his face.

old addition to Jim's pack, makes up for me and lingers back, telling me he'll find something for me even if the pack has cleared the buffet.

Now Zeb, another of Gary's pointing retrievers, grew ill in the kennel truck during the 18-hour trip from Parker, Colorado, to Kamiah, Idaho. So he was off his game the entire week and warranted all our concern and well wishes.

Boo, Butch's great young male Chessie, went to field the way Butch used to play linebacker. He got a volunteer flyer, and chased it to the horizon. Since the bird couldn't really fly, it could only labor just above the grass tops. Butch couldn't shoot because the bird was so low and Boo wouldn't veer. To have any one of these men's dogs sleep in my bed and walk in my quail fields would be better than winning the lottery.

THE MAN FROM MARS

If you could have the objectivity of a man from Mars, a man who had never seen gun dog work before and could only wonder

174

Jim Charlton sees cock pheasant volunteer before Sage's relentless press. An unusual picture for bird to be in focus while dog and hunter are blurred.

what on earth those mortals and those animals were doing chasing those birds, you could come to some unbiased and logical conclusions.

So that's the role I took. As a Martian I could tell Jim Charlton was self-conscious. Why not? He's the stranger here. All these other guys have been knocking about for 10 years. Plus he's never played the game this loose before: let the dog self-cast? Let the dog hunt without command?

Jim's dogs sensed this and were not solid. It was not that they are poor dogs. Far from it. It was that they were concerned about their buddy and wondered why he was feeling the way he was. Dogs know. Dogs are intuitive. Dogs read our minds.

175

This picture is important because it shows what Gary Ruppel means by influence handling. You see him move right and his dogs do likewise. It's body movement that prompts direction change for the pack. When Gary went to field at Kamiah, his dogs were directed in some parts of their hunt by their handler.

So in the first runs, these goldens lacked the intensity I saw them exhibit when they worked before me on Sauvie Island in Portland, Oregon.

Mike, I feel, didn't like the setup, so he didn't work the bird critically. Also, Web thought it was a ridiculous marking test with all the photographers afield, and he told Mike, "I don't like this."

Mike is a stickler about not presenting anything afield that can be interpreted as phony to a dog. Mike says dogs know when you're playing games. They say, "When did we start doing this stuff?"

THE HUNT BRUSHED ASIDE

It was demanded the test be scrapped, and no matter how *avant garde*, how libertarian, we want to be, the group opted to run a typical field trial test. Field trials are an infection, you see. You get to knowing field trials and vying in field trials, and it gets in your blood like dirt gets under your nails.

176

No matter how hard you try to come clean, to break away, to curse all the bad things about field trials that too often prompt brutal training, nevertheless, given the chance, you'll plant a 300 yard blind, you'll set up an angle-water entry for a training dummy, you'll have the dogs run over the spot where the previous test had the bird boys lay down the bird bag. Banished to the salt pits is the dog who honors this scent.

FIELD TRIAL TRICKS

It's all tricks, dirty tricks. Tricks that deny natural work, natural dogs. Tricks that demand, instead, mechanical dogs. Dogs that can deny their instincts to excel in this deceiving game that men want to play.

So here we are, setting up a field trial test with a stream running down the middle, but that doesn't detract anything for me. I still have the dogs to watch and the handlers to ponder.

GOING TO WATER

This water thing was a consensus test. The whole gang contributed to its design. Everything was short, nothing over 40 feet. But once again, as per field trial rigidity, the dog was not to hunt for the bird, he was instead to be a canine mortician, and he was not to find a bird to shoot: he was to find a dead bird to fetch.

Thus, the handler is on the north side of the bank with the dog at heel. A bird boy is on the south side of the bank with a popper and bird.

Both men start walking west at the same time. The bird boy fires a blank and tosses the bird, so we have a mark. Well, in a way we do. You see, at an actual field trial, the dog's handler would whistle the dog to sit. Then he would cast him with a directional back, but not here. The dog is already working to front, so it's up to the dog. Some start toward the creek while others go down but change their mind and come back up.

Once again, it's fascinating for me to see what the handlers do. Jim Charlton hits his golden with the whistle before he enters the water. This destroys the dog's concentration, throws him completely off balance and out of synch. Now the golden mismarks the single and just generally does a bad job.

If you think I'm picking on Jim, I'm not. Jim's dogs are superb. It's just that we must remember Jim came to this workshop cold: he'd not met one of these men in his life. He only knew me. He sensed something happening here that is very radical, very new and strange and different. He wonders how he'll be viewed with his classic approach, that's all.

INTERFERENCE WITH THE DOG'S RUNNING

We see it happen again and again. Anytime the handler interferes with the dog by blowing a whistle, the dog blows the test, which proves again what I've been saying all along. Leave the dog alone; let him hunt on his own; let him be his own free agent.

It was some 30 years ago that I had a friend qualify for a national running. He had a good dog, and he could win, but not if he kept that whistle in his mouth. I told him, "Cram that whistle, you hear me? Throw it away…that would be the best thing to do. But don't blow it. Don't ever blow it."

Silently, this friend and his dog became the national champs for that year.

He called me long distance late that night–after the party. And through the vapors of booze I could hear him saying, "Thank you, Bill, for telling me about that whistle. I didn't know. I owe you."

BUT WHAT ABOUT GARY'S WHISTLE TRAINING?

Now, you could well charge that Gary blows his whistle all the time to enhance the work of his retrievers. How then, can whistle blowing cause a retriever to mess up on a bird?

Well, all whistles are not created equal. When a handler blows a sit whistle (one loud and abrupt blast), that dog is going to sit. He's going to flop like brain shot and with a hole through the brain, whatever he was thinking about blew out his ear.

But Gary's whistle is an entreating whistle. It is a whistle of joy and encouragement. It is a location whistle so the dog knows where the handler is. It is a steadying whistle, a support whistle.

There is that difference, then, and all dogs know it. Just like they know the difference between "whoa" and "no." The words sound alike but the dogs never mistake the two.

Jim Charlton and Sage approach water test. Dog has left handler's side and is hunting on his own.

THE WATER TEST

Okay back to our water single. We don't have a dog entering a scent cone, knocking up game, nor working wing and shot.

The ancient field trial beat goes on. All dogs work well on this setup. But wait–

Now someone wants a blind to follow the single mark. A blind? We've already agreed a hunting retriever seldom runs a blind. Jim Charlton runs a duck club on his property. He has some six to nine gunners a day, three days a week. I asked him how many blinds he runs. He said, "About once a week."

Now let's put a pencil to that. Say there's an average of 7 gunners at Jim's duck club, and each of them shoot 6 times an outing. That's 42 shots a day times three days, which is 126, which means that there is one blind run for every 126 shots. Why then, do field trials and test hunts in a four series trial have two blinds? A blind should only come up at a field trial every 126 birds. See how field trials do not duplicate a day's hunt afield? Sure you do.

179

But I'm going to tell you something fellows. If we, as deep-died but newly dedicated, pros have this hard a time breaking the old field trial mold, then what chance does the average guy have of doing it?

Why in the hell can't we just let the dogs hunt? There's no answer because I'm screaming in my own head. All dogs do well on the blind, so it's to the lodge and the day is ended.

However, one thing happens I want to mention. Gary's magnificent Scarlet does not want anything to do with water. Why should she? Just down from the high altitudes of cold Colorado where she's been frolicking in the snow, how could she have been introduced to water?

But after we all get home and many written pages have flowed through this keyboard, Gary and I talk on the phone and he tells me he took Scarlet to a pond and he disrobed and the two of them skinny-dipped together. Now Scarlet doesn't want to play land games any more. Scarlet wants to keep her tresses sleek and wet.

But I almost forgot Scarlet and the pepper grass pheasant. She came from the truck and swept the field telling everyone how great they were, and that she wasn't too bad herself. Then Gary directed her to the field and gave her a cast. She whooped it up, made a great sashay or two, them WHAM she had the bird, it popped up, and she took off in pursuit, and Gary fired his training pistol. The price just went up on Scarlet.

As it also did on Camas, Mike Gould's infant prodigy. Oh how three years from now I'd love to put these two female shooting retrievers up against the national field trial champion. They'd leave him (her?) naked in the field. You who read this, or field trialers who wouldn't touch this book with a dip stick, hear about this: let's set this hunt up. Okay? Oh God, let me live to see a befuddled national champ with his dumbfounded handler.

BACK AT THE LODGE

That night at the lodge I was handed the most valuable insight into our outing when Butch Goodwin and Mike Gould started a running skirmish on how much control was necessary to run a shooting retriever.

You'll remember that I have told you to just let the dogs go. To run them in packs and let them self learn, to never direct them, to let them come up like wild Indians. Don't ever forget Ben Williams and his prairie Brittanies, okay? Well, that's exactly how Mike trains his personal dogs and more than most clients know, that's how their dogs are brought along as well, if possible.

But Butch? We all know Butch. He's out of that rigid framework of the field trial game where dogs are forced to do impossible things afield, like run between two bushes five feet apart and 300 yards out. Yes, a totally dominated retriever can be driven through that constricted a space, but it demands taking all options away from the dog.

I am suddenly witness to two men in a vital debate. One pro who's training life is based on the philosophy that you let dogs do what their natural instincts declare, and the other pro who knows that dogs must do what they're told.

For a running commentary, and possibly the most valuable material in this book, turn to the next chapter.

But One Moment

You must remember these were preserve birds. Consequently, harken back to what Gary Ruppel told us. He said, "The pointing retrievers came about because of game preserves where the birds didn't fly, because pointing retrievers sight point…they look down at the game." And that's what we saw here in Kamiah.

The best work across the board was posted by the pointing retrievers, and that's that.

Individual stellar performances were posted by the nonpointers who have long been legends, but they would excel no matter what field they entered.

※

The Shooting Retriever's Great Debate

Butch, a Mac truck with a load of Chessies on the Honda highway of life, and Mike, who walks barefoot with mountain spirits and let's his gun dogs determine their own Karma—they meet in the best two falls out of three, and I've got the popcorn concession.

We have a debate here about training, but really, it's our introduction on how to hunt upland game with shooting retrievers.

Butch is talking. Butch is always talking. He's not the tall, silent type. Butch talks loud and sometimes he gets demonstrative with his hands and waves his arms and, all in all, appears formidable: excited and formidable.

Butch is communicative in all things. He sends me reams of stuff out of his computer. A recent mailing, printed in bold, black, block letters, tells me, "If there is one thing that I am an expert on, it's my own opinion."

Butch also takes time to instruct me on how to become a better writer. He has told me George Bernard Shaw said, "Good writers borrow. Great writers steal."

Now he's telling all the dog pros present, "Ol' Maggie, God bless her, was a totally electrically shock-trained dog. You know, teaching her backs and hand signals.

"But this morning after those pheasants, I had a little dog out that's really never had a collar on, and what I'm seeing," says Butch, "is the performance was a lot better than what the shock-

One of Mike's Labs meets force with force as he breaches the water on retrieve. I remember accompanying Mike when he'd throw his whole pack into the raging Roaring Fork River at Carbondale, Colorado. The current would sometimes sweep the dogs a quarter mile downstream. But whitewater, not farm ponds, makes a water dog.

trained dog can do. I've got to admit it." Butch is also one to repeat himself. "Yes, I've got to admit it."

He continues talking. He's got the floor and if anyone can move 300 pounds of bone, muscle, lanyard, whistle, and check cord, they can have it. Butch is telling everyone, "That dog I trained without the collar, he's more solid and everything. You know, you take the collar off a shock-trained dog and he goes berserk.

"The pup that's been brought along with sensitivity is solid before and after a mistake or a success. Not with a collar-trained dog. If he makes a mistake, he knows it's going to be hell to pay, and he lives a life of anxiety."

184

I can't believe what I'm hearing. Butch is delivering Dogdom's Sermon on the Mount. I never thought I'd hear it.

He changes the subject, as he says, "Of all the retrievers that hunt, forget about those that just sit in the back of a Volvo. All the ones that hunt are used primarily for waterfowl.

"I'm a waterfowl hunter. I hunted ducks 62 days last year and pheasant only 15. You know, when the duck population dropped, you'd be amazed how many hunters who you would have thought would be solid sportsmen…these guys said, with no more ducks, then it's not worth the trouble to train a retriever."

THE TERM RETRIEVER CHEAPENS THE NAME

Butch takes a swig of soda pop, which gives Mike Gould a chance to slip in, "I don't like that word retriever. When you speak of goldens, Labs, Chessies…fine, but when you put retriever behind their name, that cheapens the dog. They are not retrievers, they are shooting dogs.

"They are capable of doing so much more than just fetch birds. They can do it all. They can hunt any bird, in any field or marsh, and they will find it for you, lift it for your gun, and then bring it to hand. So the fetching is so little of what they can do."

THE CLIENTS

"Yeah," says Butch, "but my clients…they're thinking just that. Their primary need is for that dog to find the bird in high tules, that CRP up to your shoulders. They want me to train them a retriever, and they want a dog they can control."

"Well, that's the old way," concurs Mike. "But it's up to us, as both the dog and the hunter's helper, to expand the retriever's role, and assuredly Butch, control ain't the way to do it."

Butch tries to protest, to take the floor back, but Mike surges on. You've got to know this about Mike: he talks soft and slow, like Jimmy Stewart or Gray Cooper, and sometimes you have to cup a hand behind an ear to even hear him.

Mike says, "We have this fabulous opportunity to change things training for the public, working directly with the hunter. For example, I'll do this commonly, someone will come in and say,

This is the most important chapter in this book. Maybe the most important chapter I ever wrote. Here's burly Butch Goodwin, who says the control's got to be in the dog before you can take him to birds.

And here's Mike Gould, who says, "Not so. If you don't put the birds in first, you'll never have a bird dog.

'Okay you had my dog for three or four months, and I'm having trouble doing this, or doing that, or one thing or the other.'

TAKING THE CLIENT TO FIELD

"I'll say, 'Okay, let's go out to the field here, and we'll make sure there's some birds in the area…and I'll make you a deal. You can't talk to the dog. You can't blow your whistle, or say anything, or do anything. You will have to become invisible. No funny stuff. Okay?

"A half hour out there in that field with their dog and the light comes on. For neither of us has given the dog a command. We have let him have his own head to do his own thing. If he wants to look for birds, so be it. If he wants to run to the skyline, let him go. Whatever he wants to do, let him.

"But in a half hour, he will become the gun dog everyone wants. He will have gotten all that run out of him, and all the need to express himself, and now he's ready to work. So it's like a religious experience for the client.

"You see the real flaw...and Bill and I talk about this a lot...the real flaw in humanity is man's desire to control. That is the basic flaw. We just have this natural desire to control, and our dogs bear the brunt of this."

DOMINATION IN GUN DOG TRAINING IS DEAD

Mike looks to me to see if I want to offer anything. I tell the group, "Domination in gun dog training is dead. Mike has proven that if you let the dog have his head in the field, the dog will provide his own control."

Butch leaps in before Mike can speak. He blurts out, "You two guys! Don't you think a little control is necessary?" His voice is up a half octave.

I say, "The dog will provide the control. Right now, the human thinks he has to do it. I want the dog to provide it."

Mike says, "And one thing I like about what Bill says, Butch. I think I can prove that influence handling is not only more powerful than electricity, it's more permanent."

Each of us in this group has a different word for training with our head, not our hand...for giving the dog every latitude so he can express himself...for each of us to get all the dog out of the dog. I call it bonding. Mike and Gary call it influence handling. Whatever it is called, it means the dog is trained with respect and humanity. Mike has learned that whatever way you move in a field, the dog will duplicate it. That's influence handling: the movement influences the dog.

Butch surprises us all by answering Mike's assertion that kindness in training is more lasting and more effective than using electricity to accomplish what you seek. He says simply, "I don't disagree with that."

Butch has been out there 10 years with that electric collar, and now he is saying, "I don't disagree with that."

I'm so proud of Butch. I can see he's struggling. It's something to admit to yourself you've been wrong. It's something to admit it before those people you respect the most.

I want to help Butch so I confess, "In *The Magic of Dogs*, which is a family dog book, I ask the reader to not train his dog. That's right, not train it. And the reason for that is this. If a guy who's never been around a dog and who knows nothing about commu-

Here's the author's pack of wild Indians stopped to honor dog on extreme left as he smells something that's stopped him.

nicating with it starts giving commands, the dog can view the person as the heavy. I don't want these dogs intimidated. Plus, by osmosis...just by living with you...that dog's going to learn everything in three years he'd have learned if he'd been sent to a pro trainer. I'm convinced of this because I've proven this.

"I have an experiment in my own home right now with two dogs who have not been trained. Never a heel, sit, stay. These dogs are two years old now, and you'd think they had gone to college. They just learned it from my thinking it, and they learned it from emulating the other house dogs.

VALUE OF BASIC DISCIPLINE

"But...and this is the point I want to make. I say never give a dog an order. I say let the dog self-learn. Yet Mike has now proven to me a dog must have basic discipline. That's right. As much as we want these dogs to operate with minimum control, nevertheless, when the gun dog goes off his game, Mike returns him to basic yard work, and the dog immediately straightens up."

"That's right," confirms Mike, "when a dog turns me off, the way I restore the desired performance is I take the dog back to basic yard drills, which means there has to be that initial control."

I butt in, "You see I wanted to do away with that initial control. You must understand this. You guys have a clientele. Maybe 10 men, maybe 50, whatever, and to a certain point you know what they are going to do with that dog. Me? I'm a writer-trainer. I send the magazine columns, and I send the books out to millions of people. There is no way I can imagine what the average person is going to do with what I write. I've got to be so careful. I can't write anything that could be misconstrued and get a dog hurt. So I go overboard asking for kindness and understanding, for patience and love."

Butch says, "The electric collar never hurt a dog, its the idiot who hits the button."

I tell him, "I don't care how you cut it or what you believe. I just flat don't want the dog hurt. I've put that collar around my own neck and hit the button. It flat damn hurts. A dog is too great a gift from God to abuse."

Jim Charlton breaks a long silence to say, "There's a place for certain dogs with that collar in training. Smart animals don't need it."

I reply, "Forget the collar...I'm really concerned about the 7-week-old pup being destroyed the first day of adoption by someone who doesn't realize how heavy he comes on."

Gary says, "As dog trainers, those are the guys we are trying to communicate with. Let those pups have a little love. Treat them like a child."

"You'll have more control of the dog if you do," I offer. "That's with a love-trained dog, a dog that's bonded with his human partner. Why, a disappointed look on the handler's face hurts the bonded dog more than if you hit the traditionally trained dog with a 2x4."

THE CROSS THE PRO BEARS

"Yeah," says Butch, "but what are you going to do with the typical pro's bring-on dog? He's sat in a kennel for a year, and now all of a sudden his owner brings him to you and wants him trained in three months. In three months I don't have time to bond. Love-trained? What are you going to do with the dog that's untrainable?"

Mike tells him, "Well Butch, you take a dog like that, and I know there's a ton of problems connected with it. But listen. If you train your dogs for total compliance, your program is going to fail. But if you train for total confidence, your program will ultimately be successful. So that stimulus-deprived dog that's sat sterile in a yard a year…first you've got to give him self-worth and from that will come confidence. He can be trained."

Butch says, "I'll buy that."

And Gary offers, "Develop that control through positive conditioning. Nothing negative."

Mike says, "I really believe in control, Butch. But I honestly believe all we have to do is have the ability to read our dogs. Powers of control are out there without us putting them into the dog. We must just be able to read what is controlling our dogs as they run across the field."

IF YOU EVER WANT A BIRD DOG

"However, it is imperative we let these dogs hunt as babies. Then later, you can put the handle on them…the controls…if that's what you want. But control first and never hunt, and you'll never have a bird dog.

"If you put the handle on your dog first, then he'll never be the bird dog he could have been, because he will never have the power of youth, the power of being out there searching and finding birds on his own. And you develop that natural ability. Now you can still take that dog and put the handle on him later.

"But look at the opposite. Take a dog that's been handled early and has the control embedded…you'll never put the birds in later."

Gary says, "That's right. I don't know haw many dogs I've seen come into my kennels that were taught heel, sit, stay, and when I teach them to hunt a bird, they are bootlickers. They won't leave my feet."

HOW TO STOP A PUP FROM EATING A BIRD

Butch says, "There's something here I don't understand."

Gary asks openly, "Chessies?"

"No," says Butch, "What I don't understand is how you guys keep those pups from eating those birds."

191

Mike tells Butch, "We shoot a bird for a pup. The pup grabs it and takes off, so what do you do? Let's say he's going to lay down and eat it. Know what I do?

"I go the other way and I look at the sky, and I think about the clouds and I think, boy it's a heck of a day. And I start thinking about other things, and before you know it, that pup's got the bird right in front of me.

"The puppy will make that adjustment. For you know what's at stake here, what's involved here? *You first have to take the pressure off the pup for him to have the latitude to make the adjustment you want.*"

And folks, that's what I mean by training with your head, not your hand. By training with intimacy, not intimidation.

I tell Mike, "What you're saying is disconnect the bond, and the pup demands you re-establish it."

Gary tells us, "People. They don't let the dog have the value of being what he is. You ever see 'em? They shoot a bird and run after it yelling, 'I got it, I got it.' They'll beat the poor dog to the bird. They never ran that fast in high school track."

Butch looks about the room and says in a declaratory voice, "Due to this discussion, I will now consider taking a pup through that relaxed bird introduction and constant commitment."

We hear dinner being called and head up the stair steps that are half-trunks with the bark beneath. I look back at the great lodge room. You know your household fireplace has a fire screen with three sections. The Flying B's fireplace is so massive, the screen has nine sections. On the walls are sporting prints. On the floor are pelts.

We sit at a great round table ladened with fresh, sweet corn. Remember Garrison Keillor wrote in the intro to one of his great books that he was telling his wife at dinner he thought sweet corn was better than sex?

Everyone reaches first for the sweet corn. Then there are string beans and steaks and huge salad makings and fresh bread and slabs of butter and iced tea. We all gained at least six pounds that week. Even our running up and down mountains after black bear couldn't keep the weight down.

After dinner the sun has gone down, the lodge has a lantern-glow to it, and we sink back into overstuffed chairs in the great room and I thought we'd all fall asleep. But no, Butch has been thinking.

Mike wants his dogs to experience everything in nature. Here he waits for the Roaring Fork to flood and casts his pack to whitewater.

RUNNING TO HELL AND GONE OR WITHIN GUN RANGE

He says, "About this control, Mike. You let your dogs run big, and I keep my Chessies within gun range. You've previously told me you don't care if your dogs knock birds...and that's because you're hunting chukar, for example, that will usually fly downhill to where you're waiting with a gun. But tell me, what are you going to do with those knocked birds on the flat? There is no hill for them to come down."

INFLUENCE HANDLING

"I take care of that with influence handling," answers Mike. "Where you start out with puppies influencing them back and forth, left and right. That is, you walk one of those ways and the

Here they all go south, but Mike throws sticks behind them which prompts three to turn about and beat back up current.

pup does the same. Then as the months go by, he mirrors every step you take.

"So if the shooting dog gets too far out for gun range on flat ground, I let them cast out and I either stop or I back up, and they come back toward me.

"Now, if the wind's just right I shoot 60 percent of my birds flying right at me, and that's with a dog out there working at extreme distances. Because I like to get the dog on flat ground looping out and driving back toward me, and the only way that can come about is if they cast a long ways."

Remember Ben Williams and the brilliant Winston? Ben and his Brittany were also sandwiching Hungarian partridge, and the dog drove them to the gun.

Butch asks, "What about Nebraska or Kansas...wide fields of row crops and pheasants?"

"Fine," answers Mike, "let's hope there are five hundred birds in there. My ideal hunt would be to to go through that field and see all five hundred pheasants and kill three of them. That's why I love to hunt the Labs from horseback. I just don't think they can cast too far...if they're going to drive the birds back to you."

"But Boo…" says Butch, referring to Maggie's pup—

But Mike predicts the question and offers, "Let's say you're riding through this field right now on horseback and Boo is out there one hundred and seventy five yards. Okay? You see he starts getting birdy, and you just go tweet. And then you ride over there, dismount, walk up and say, 'Git in there,' and boom, boom, boom."

Butch protests saying, "Most hunters don't know enough to let a dog go like that: 175 yards. These guys have never heard of influence handling and probably wouldn't believe it if they saw it. They don't know that as handlers they can stop or go forward and influence the dog to do the same. All most of 'em know is, 'Git in here…damn it…git in here.'

"That's why I put my clients' dogs under control before I let them roll, so I can, in fact, go beep and stop them."

THE POPULAR WAY OF DOING IT

"Well definitely, that's the popular way of doing it," grants Mike. "But by doing that, I think it takes the bird dog right of your dog. You'll end up with a pretty good working dog, but he's not a shooting dog like I want. For the only way a dog can ever become a shooting dog and develop their aptitude and ability is to run wild for one whole year."

Butch tells Mike, "Your talking about keeping a dog for a year, and you've got a multi-thousand acre game preserve here for them to run in. Me? I get a dog for three months, and I've got to be very careful where they run."

Mike answers, "'When you put on a lot of pressure to handle a dog—you know, incessant commands—it creates mental fatigue for the animal, which is much more tiring than physical fatigue. No man wants a boss hanging over his shoulder. So the ideal situation is to go out there and relax physically and mentally, and this will extend their endurance more than you can believe.

THE LOOPER

"Anyway, I think if your dog learns to loop out and hunt back, it teaches him to manipulate birds. And when you get into those ditches, or into those tall tules, and stuff like that, it's no longer a sight thing. The dog and you then switch over to some kind of mental telepathy hook-up. I don't know if anybody knows what it really is. But that dog knows exactly where you are, exactly what you're doing, and exactly what you want him to do."

"Yes," says Butch, "but you misunderstand. My problem is not the dogs. My problem is the people."

A Bitch Named Pal

Mike says, "What I do with the people is I tell them, 'Let's talk about this control.' Give you an example with Doug Boyle. You remember Doug? He had a wild, wild dog, just a beautiful young Labrador. One of Web's kids, just a wild woman. And he got to Kansas and he'd hear the same story from everybody. When you going to put a shock collar on that dog? You need to start puttin' some control on that little girl. And Doug would come back to me and he'd say, 'Gee I didn't know what to do, my friends are mad out there at me and everything. My dog's running so big. There's no control.'

"I told him, drop her off and meet me out at the bird pen tomorrow evening and bring your wife. And I told him to leave the dog with me. I didn't do one thing with that dog except for about ten minutes of obedience the next morning. And when we got to the ranch, we went to the bird pen.

"Now, I mean this dog is wild, crazy. She'd kick all the birds out of the country, just absolutely bird crazy.

"So we're there by the bird pen, and I tell Doug and his wife, we've got to make a deal now. You can't laugh or wave your arms, call to her, or try to get cute, or anything. I just want you to think about what's going on. So this little female Lab, her name was Pal, and I walked into the bird pen. I told Pal, heel…on lead…sit, stay. And we walked right out into the middle of that bird pen, and I told her to sit.

"I'm taking the lead off her and I'm telling her, now I don't want you moving.

"Then I walked her around that pen, and she just stared at me. She was oblivious to birds forming clouds of feather right before her eyes, and she just kept staring at me. And the only thing I did was just show her some structure. Some structure with yard drills.

When pups can walk they're started on nature walks. What's that sight? What's that odor? What's that noise?

"Okay, it seems like magic, and you can always say, yeah, *you* can do that, but what about me? Well, I've noticed that the ladies are particularly good with this. I think the important thing, Butch is you talk to the owners when they come in or the people you're out hunting with. Tell them, get off control. I can prove that influence handling is not only more powerful than electricity, it's also more permanent.

"You can cast your English pointers out there a half mile without saying a word. And sure, it's a little weird, and it's such an angle they don't believe you at first, but if you do take your owners out there and you handle the dog all over the field without saying a word, or doing anything but walking, it's impressive enough they'll go ahead and follow up on it.

"Just take a good rider," says Mike. "He looks like he's just sitting there, looks like he's doing nothing. And that's the really good one. And the good dog handler, he looks like he's doing nothing, too.

197

Butch does advocate control, as evidenced by this walk-up at a test hunt. Dog must remain at heel; they're not freed to search out birds and knock them to sky.

HE DOESN'T TRAIN, HE JUST FOLLOWS 'EM AROUND

"I had an employee here for awhile, and he went down to south Texas and the pros down there asked him, 'What's this Mike like? How does he train?' And this guy told them, 'All he does is follow the dogs around.' He was here a year and had no idea of what I was doing. It's simple. If you can influence your dog to proper behavior, it's one hundred times better than disciplining your dog to proper behavior."

Butch is squirming. He wants to believe Mike but...finally, he says, "I feel like your letting a dog kick up birds 125 yards out makes as much sense as throwing 125 yard marks at a field trial."

Mike comes right back at him, declaring, "It's totally diametrically opposite. Take grouse on the flat tops. Let's say your Boo is out there hunting blue grouse at 300 yards.

"There's a covey of 7 or 9 birds, okay? Boo is going to hit that covey and three birds are going to go. That'll be momma and a couple of poults. Now your dog is going to try and run those birds down. Okay?

198

"Now, what you do as a handler, rather then be cussing out Boo, is try this. Walk directly to where that flush came because you know in your heart there's three to five more grouse sitting there. As soon as you get near to where you think the covey is, you wait and Boo will chase down there a ways and bounce to a stop. He'll stand there and watch the birds sail over the rim. Then he comes back up over the hill.

"When he gets to you, you tell him, 'Git in there,' and two more birds will go, and Boo will chase them 15 yards. But the third time you send him in, he'll bounce to a stop as they leave, for he's learned he can't catch them.

"So I think," concludes Mike, "flushing birds at extreme distances teaches your dog to get back in there."

Gary jumps in saying, "Not only that but you see so many more birds with a dog that's rolling. You walk past so many birds if you're holding your dog to 30 yards."

WHAT GOOD ARE THEY?

Butch say in exasperation, "So you see lots of birds...what good are they 250 yards out? I can't buy it. Letting dogs knock birds that far out is as ridiculous as throwing 250 yard marks at a field trial."

Mike smiles as he tells Butch, "My dog just knocked 25 pheasant from a sumphole over there. That suggests to me, let's start hunting sumpholes, for we're hunting the wrong cover.

"Or we're out here working some good looking stubble, but my dog is knocking out birds on the hedge right now. We better shift to the hedge. In other words, the wide-ranging dog is showing you where the birds are.

"And I don't deny, Butch, that I do bump a bunch of birds out there. I do. But let me tell you when those birds come buzzing over your clients' heads from 300 yards out, it's so impressive they never forget it."

Jim Charlton has remained silent, he's been listening. Finally he says, "This natural stuff must have something to it. I have seen what Mike's talking about with that Camas and Gary's Scarlet. I'm 60 years old, and I've been running dogs for 30 years professionally, and I've had dogs of my own since I was 9. And I was just amazed at what those two little bitches can do. I thought I knew it all." Everyone agrees with Jim's assessment.

This trainer wants his dogs birdy, so he tantalizes them with a big, cock pheasant.

Then someone observes, "You see how those dogs got fouled up today when the handler blew that whistle?"

Mike answers, "You've got to train the dog with the whistle to bring him up to bond, but you no longer blow it while hunting because it stops the dog short and takes away his initiative."

JAY KNOWS SHOOTING RETRIEVERS

Mike thinks a moment, then changes the subject, offering, "I asked Jay…" (Jay is one of Mike's six associate dog trainers. He's new, fresh, and has no preconceived notions.) "I asked Jay," says Mike, "which dog here today was the hardest to handle. He said the Chesapeake. I said which one is the hardest to keep in close? 'Well no doubt,' he said, 'the Chessie.' Then I said, isn't it odd that he's the only one that is completely electric-shock trained? If there was supposed to be a push-button dog, don't you think that would be him? I think it's a graphic illustration that the damned shock collar doesn't work. Plus it's temporary…

This bobwhite hunter walks an exhausted German shorthair pointer and a Lab out of the field with quail enough to feed his family.

"Take the collar off an electrically-trained dog and tomorrow he will have 80 percent of his efficiency. A month from now he will have 60 percent, and in three months, he'll be lucky to have 25 percent. Unless you go back to the collar program with that dog, you'll never get back to 20 percent efficiency the rest of his life."

A LOT OF VALUE FOR HUNTING UPLAND GAME

The group continues talking, but after Mike's declaration, what's there left to say? I stand, say good night, and go to bed.

I can't remember when a discussion of professional gun dog trainers was ever reported before. Fascinating, really.

I don't know what each of these pros got out of their evening, but I feel a benefit exists there—both in training and hunting for upland game—that is surely yours.

SUMMING UP

The last three chapters have been vital: there we started taking our VSRs for upland game. While our sensitivity gang remained at the Flying B, we went to field again, this time seeding the area so each dog would have multiple birds to scent.

Production was still nil: little scent, no breeze, fumigating chlorophyll odor, high heat, and searing sun. But again the dogs did a creditable job. If it had been a hunt for dinner, all of us would have left the table full.

It was never my intent, nor would it have served any purpose, to report what we did at Kamiah as though it were a field trial. It was a workshop, and I was photographing each dog and was enthused—I can hear myself yelling in my tape recorder, "That's beautiful...just beautiful."

So the documentary TV that was shot of our field work may show I misreported one dog's work or another. Again, that's not of interest. What mattered was all dogs self-cast, worked the field, sought scent, some found it, many retrieved a shot bird, others chased a flyaway, and some trailed a runaway to no end. In other words we did see—even though two of the trainers are waterfowl specialists—that any basically trained retriever can be a VSR.

Now to the field and to the game bird. Let's go.

Hunting for Upland Game

*It was a long time ago. I was driving a farm-to-
market road and stopped. Rolling the window
down, I asked the boy, "You finding any birds?"
He was matter of fact in answering, "No, but
my dog is." Remember this! It's the dog that
finds the bird, not you. Help him.*

For the last three chapters we've entered the upland bird field. The essential lesson learned was this: you either 1) enter the scent cone with a retriever that'll point, whoa, or produce a delayed flush on command, or 2) you cast the retriever far out to loop back and drive the bird to the gun.

These two methods were amply discussed by control-minded Butch Goodwin and let-freedom-ring retriever trainer Mike Gould. So that's how we do it, but what are the particular strategies, how are they accomplished, and what of the dog?

THE UPLAND GAME RETRIEVER

The upland game retriever must have thrust and independence. He must have a big motor in him (her) to self-hunt, and the self-initiative to cast, sustain a drive, and tenaciously stick to it until he produces feather.

It takes a dog with: *heart, stamina, brilliance, birdiness, athletic prowess, biddability, high pain threshold, perfect physical condition, and love of game.*

It takes intensity; dogs that are bird nuts; dogs that won't eat for three days prior to a season's start.

We're going to take this dog after most upland game. However, some birds are nearly impossible to hunt with any species of dog–I'm thinking now of mountain quail. These birds are usually harvested as the result of the gunner seeking something else and the mountain quail flying into the line of fire.

When possible, we're going to put the dog on the bird in more ways than one. But no matter the species of bird, there are general rules to hunting and let's see what they are.

THE FUNDAMENTALS OF BIRD-DOM

No matter what bird is being hunted, we always work into the wind. Of course, Ben Williams and his prairie Brittanies had a special importance for working crosswind. Be that as it may, we don't ever hunt with the wind. That would be as unproductive as shoveling clam shells into a tidal wave. Plus, we always work point of objectives.

OBJECTIVES

The primary objective is the edge. Ninety percent of all birds are found within ten percent of the edge of any field or flora complex. I'll explain.

A change in cover can be very subtle and escape the tyro's eye, like a large cottonwood tree in a dense, grass field. The perimeter of that tree is an edge. Or a sand plum thicket in a pasture. The circumference of that thicket is an edge.

Other edges are the likely ones: road ditches, plowed furrows, hedgerows, stands of sunflowers, the shores of ponds and tanks and streams and lakes.

Never overlook an abandoned farm house, barn, school, or church. Bobwhite love the ecosystem next to the foundation of these structures, even a structure as small as a windmill.

Now, why this thing with the edge? Well, a good edge will provide the following necessities for a bird.

THE VITALS

Most birds seek overstory (a natural canopy to keep the hawks from seeing, and therefore, killing them). They also seek moisture, not necessarily to drink, but to harvest the plants and insects that frequent such a mini-ecosystem.

Mother birds likewise prefer sparsely vegetated earth, so she can get her children to food and then back to protection without getting them wet. Plus, all the birds can dust there. Just belly in, shiver all over, and let the dust penetrate the least follicle. Consequently, you'll never find a bobwhite in the middle of a sedge field and damn seldom in the middle of a CRP layout. Now those two statements will save you from some unproductive walking.

You can also maximize your harvest by knowing what birds crave. They too, have their chocolate madness.

Take doves (not an upland game bird, for certain), who can't resist popcorn or sesame. And bobwhite–the hours I've sat and listened to the late John Olin of Winchester fame tell the late John Bailey of Quail Hills Plantation, Coffeeville, Mississippi, that corn was the only feed for quail. Bailey would counter, "With all due respect, sir, it's the bicolor lespedeza they prefer." Both were right.

I've seen many occasions in a corn field when incoming mallards (admittedly not an upland game bird) couldn't be shot away.

If the lovely Mearns quail (an upland game bird of the lower Sonoran desert) loses the nut from his nut grass, it's "*Adios Amigo..*" you're dead.

KNOWING THE BIRD'S LARDER

So, one objective for you and your shooting retriever is the favorite food of the game bird you seek. Consequently, you must know the bird before nature entitles you to find and shoot him. And that's justifiable, right?

I so love nature. Seeing things there or learning things there gives me the thrill of Christmas or falling in love or getting a new pup. When Gary Ruppel called me Yoda there was no way I could understand him. I don't go to movies or bars or bowling allies.

I want what I do to have an open sky above it and grass under it. I want it to have things fly over me and run by me that I have totally no control over. When I play I don't want to hear a gasoline engine. The wind in the sail of a boat is a plus. Or hang gliding can even be accepted. But never anything mechanical or with a motor.

I turn on TV and 60 mad men are hurtling around an oval track with the entrails of their machines screaming, and then two or six of them crash into a wall and wheels fly to sky and I wonder, what the hell? Certainly, this has to be an insanity.

They could be on a lake bank or a rivulet or high up looking down from a stone ledge. They could be seeing the shadows stretch across the land, smell the fecundity of the earth, and hear its loud trumpets, small shrill calls, or hushed murmuring.

That's what hunting means to me, not shooting. Training the dog is hunting. Painting the decoys is hunting. Looking for acorns to indicate squirrels, raccoons, or quail—that's hunting. You can shoot a tin can. Shooting ends the hunt. I never want the hunt to end. So you collect photos and pictures of it to hang on your den wall. You bring home strangely shaped or brightly colored rocks. Anything to remind you that you were out there. I have a horseshoe grown into that wedge where a limb meets the trunk. It shows me nature always conquers man's doin's. As does a Kansas farm house with the porch roof caving in or the pump rod going into the well casing that's rusted shut. Nature triumphing again.

So you have to excuse my wandering somtimes. It's so lovely being out there. But you're right. Back to birds.

THE WEATHER

The weather will aid or hinder your outing. Take snow. How great the shoot is on pheasant when they've burrowed under the snow, and you seek the bird's blow hole or the dog does. The field-wise dog snorts across the landing, head down, ever scanning for that emission of scent. Then in one tumultuous explosion, he dives straight into the snow bank and up erupts a mighty disturbed and squawking pheasant. Be ready. Shoot!

But it's a mighty weird bird you'll find out in the rain.

Take pheasant again. A freezing rain will weld them shut. They'll turn their back to the blizzard, the moisture will pack under their protective plumage, freeze there, and the bird will become immobile. I've stopped in western Kansas, picked them out of a ditch, laid them in the back of the pickup or wagon, and when they'd warmed up and revived, lifted the window, and let them fly away.

Now back to cover. I'm thinking of chukar.

You'll find them aloft, high on a ridge, and that ridge may be in rock. So that line of rock forms a cover but not necessarily to produce an abundance of food, which means that nature just has some birds seek certain natural phenomena.

For instance, when I lived on the farm, I'd cut and strew bright colored yarn all over the barnyard. The Baltimore orioles would pluck it up and incorporate it in the building of their nests. The technicolor nests in my elm trees were a delight to me all summer.

For that same reason, I'd plant Japanese millet and wapato duck potato in the farm pond. To go there and lay on the bank and glass through the tules at the waterbirds. There was even a pair of whistling swans that would stop three days each spring.

Around the pond shore I'd plant sumac, which has a special characteristic for quail and pheasant. It exists through most of the bitter cold and then shatters, drooping its seed to sustain the birds during that period from solid freeze to first bud.

There's just all sorts of fun if you have land. Without it, it's a damned dreary world.

WE'RE ALL BIRD-BRAIN SPECIALISTS

Each of us has a different depth of knowledge about our favorite birds. Mike Gould is untouchable when it comes to blue grouse. He has literally lived every day of a grouse's life and knows them like he knows the blemishes on the back of his hands.

Over a long period, Mike gradually realized he was finding blue grouse in male aspen groves, and that took some doing. You can't really sex an aspen tree during hunting season. You do that in the spring or summer when the tree is in bloom. The trees with the larger blossoms are the males, and that's where the grouse will congregate in the winter.

And it goes on and on. But you've got to be an expert to know this stuff. There's slim chance that Pecos, my four-year-old shooting lab, won't find a covey of bobwhite by a farm pond dam, or a seep coming from that dam, or a rimrock above a meandering spring. Yep, the quail are always there.

Like this: It took Jim Culbertson and me years before we figured out that whenever you see a cardinal, within 100 yards there'll always be a covey of bobwhite.

Facts like that come to you only after you've lived a lifetime (so your wife would tell you it's been) in the field.

The other day I heard that the widow of a famous outdoor painter was remarrying. She told this friend of mine, "And my fiancé doesn't hunt or fish." The statement revealed her long forbearance of her late husband's passion. My friend told the widow, "Well, some men aren't all that bright, you know."

So thank God you who are reading this book are bright. Else I'd have no one of any import to talk to.

One time at a dinner party (my wife so wanted to have a social life, but she'd married riffraff), the superfluous host (he had lace on his shirt cuffs) sniffed when he asked, "How can you shoot those little birds?" No longer suffering fools, I told him, "With great skill...that's how I shoot them."

I was told, "Your answer begs my indulgence."

Smiling, I replied, "Just like your shirt cuffs do for me."

My wife's social hopes came cascading down like scree on a steep mountain slope. We've not been invited to a dinner party for 18 years.

Go Back to the Introduction

Back in the introduction, I told you to take the shells out of that gun, remember? Tom Ness was shot in the back. Dr. Moore had a hole in his International floor boards.

Death isn't always that romantic. I once asked my kennel boy, 15-year-old Robby Rupp (he was a good kid), to walk down a tree-shrouded creek banging a tin pan with a stick. Jim Culbertson and I waited on Robby and the trophy buck. The three of us wore those orange vests when a crazy woman popped up out of the bush with a rifle.

Those bullets were screaming about us as she yelled, "Leave my deer alone." My God, how long had she been waiting in there? And what did she mean, "...her deer?" I bought my license from the state of Kansas, not her.

As the long-legged Robby out-paced my Mickey Rooney, runt-size legs and even Coach Culbertson's better conditioning, I reached out and jerked the orange vest from the boy's back to make him less of a target, but not my vest. I continued running blaze orange. The bullets kept sizzling. Now that's romantic, or at least, ridiculous.

The obverse is you can go down in quicksand, get shot by a hunter you never see, be struck by a car while getting gear out of the trunk, be hit with lightning, fall through a railroad bridge you're using for a shortcut, shoot a snow-clogged shotgun barrel, or worse yet, stop at the local cafe and catch ptomaine.

DEAD DOG

Even worse, you could have your Lab come across the remnants of a torn-down stolen car and lap the antifreeze, fall into a sludge pit, run onto an interstate, get gored by a bull, stomped by a stallion, or struck by a rattler. I recall a bird dog running fast, and a rattler got his left rear paw. The dog died.

But you're right, we've got to get back to hunting.

GROUP HUNTING

I generally despise group hunting. You know: "I got it." Ten men abreast in a milo field, all yelling the same thing: "I got it."

This type of hunt differs from the two I spoke of before. You know, the dog working the bird before him or going far to field, looping back, and driving the bird to the gun.

Now we've got a line of hunters interspersed with whatever gun dogs they have along, and they beat the field, driving toward a cover change–to that place where the crop meets the road, or whatever. It could be a pipeline, a hedgerow, a creek.

Other hunters, called blockers, are waiting there with their shotguns, so you end up shooting at each other with the dogs sandwiched in the line of fire. It's jolly fun.

WESTERN KANSAS

Anyway, in western Kansas, the state of my birth, hunting pheasant is akin to standing for the national anthem. You place your hand over your heart, look dutifully to the sky, and maybe a tear appears to course your cheek.

But I hate it. The only good parts are the small towns and farm-wives, who never go to bed that first night of open season. You go to the schoolhouse where they've cooked a cholesterol nightmare and you cram it in. When you get to the pheasant field, you are a cardiac time bomb.

But anyway, that food is good and those ladies are good and don't ever forget to patronize them in western Kansas. That meal they fix could well be the best part of your bird hunt.

BACK TO THE HUNT

There are stupid and there are bright ways to walk a field. With a lot of hunters it's almost all stupid.

With one or two hunters, the birds can be manipulated. Pheasants are very responsive to noise. As you walk in those crackling row crops, the birds hunker or run. But what if you just flat stop and don't breathe? Tell Pup to sit down and hush?

The wary pheasant listens. He always listens. Now this silence annoys him, so there he goes running, or he flat jumps to fly.

Or having waited so long, you might take a stalk-snapping step, and he'll panic to sky.

But that's it. You can play the bird, not with a big group, but with two or so men. Besides, before the day's out, a gang hunt raises the dust, the outing gets very hot, the dogs get clogged, their eyes puddle debris, their nose is coated dust, your feet become weary, your shins are barked by tough stubble. You've been up since 3 a.m, and you can no longer see. Your face is sunburned; your lips are cracked; the gun weighs 20 pounds. Gang hunts are no way to go.

I was invited to hunt with a bunch of guys at Stuttgart. We were all in a duck blind like rub-a-dub-dub. A duck went by and everyone barraged. They all yelled, "I got it." I yelled back, "I didn't get it."

I was disgusted. I sat in the back of the blind with a dog who wanted out, too.

One guy broke the stock on his gun and didn't realize that he had. When the next duck came by, he rammed that splintered stock into his shoulder and pulled the trigger. I was the one who took him to the hospital to get the slivers removed.

210

Gang hunts—never.

Read that book by Vance Bourjaily. Remember, Hemingway wrote he was the best writer in America or something like that. Bourjaily hunts pheasant alone. He not only writes well, he thinks well.

DOGS WORKING PHEASANTS

When walking row crops or CRP for pheasant, you will orchestrate your dog movements. My dogs have always cast obliquely, looped into the center of the field, and pushed the birds to me. Remember what Butch Goodwin said two or three chapters back about a smart dog not needing an electric collar? Well, a smart dog doesn't need anything.

A smart dog will learn all this looping by himself. But if not, I'll give you two drills to teach it. Later.

LATERALLY

It's counterproductive to ever cast a VSR laterally in a pheasant field to lift birds, since all moving birds are seeking an edge, which means escape. You'll have some vagabond pheasants come through the country. One banded Kansas cock walked halfway across the state. However, most of these birds live in that field you're hunting, or the next section, and they know the territory

There is one thing you can do that often proves productive, and that's to stop and back-cast the VSR. Send him (her) back over land you've covered. You'll be amazed how many birds have tunneled in back there and breathlessly waited for you and your dog to pass.

SHELTERBELTS

In mid-America—I hate the misnomer, the "Midwest." The Midwest would be from Denver to Salt Lake City; the mideast would be Toledo; the East would be New York; and the West would start at Tonapah, Nevada.

I've wanted to mention that for ages. Chauvinistic New Yorkers decided the nation would have no mideast. Their coastal province of the East would extend all the way to the Midwest, which in reality extended nowhere since the Midwest is actually the mideast.

Well anyway, in mid-America we hunt shelterbelts, often called hedgerows. These columns of trees (usually *bois d'arc*, also called Osage orange) are as tough a survivor and as hard to cut as ironwood trees. The birds love them. They provide all the essentials: a canopy for hawks, dirt base, minimum foliage, dust, an edge (usually a wheat crop, corn, milo, soy bean, or whatever) right there. In other words, groceries, and the hedge is also a fortress. The hunter comes on one side, the bird sneaks out the other.

That's why you hunt a hedgerow with two men and two dogs. Now the birds are yours. Many birds won't wait to walk clear to the end of the hedge and hit that edge. They panic and fly to side. You've got them. I've killed more birds in hedgerows than all other places put together. But then, you'll remember I hunt my VSRs almost exclusively on bobwhite, and bobwhite are the primary hedgerow dwellers.

PEN-RAISED OR WILD

Of course, you hunt a VSR different on a wild bird than you would on one that's been liberated. Pen-raised birds are tame birds. They hold longer for a dog, and they fly less hardy than a wild bird. They also have less gas in them to run the length of a section.

We have seen that a pointing retriever is excellent for pen-raised pheasant. These dogs are sight pointers, and they crowd the bird to see him, to know he's there. The bird does not spook, so the hunter gets a cheap shot. That's right: cheap. The bird doesn't explode as furious or as fast. He doesn't fly with deceptive speed. He doesn't know how to dupe you like a wild bird because he's never had to. He was always hand fed and was always screened away from raptors. It's the difference between hunting an African bushman and a New York welfare recipient. One's had to outwit nature to live. The other had to have the strength and wit to find the next free chow line and army cot.

I neither condemn nor make fun of the welfare guy, God bless him. No way will he ever know the joy of the open field, the flash of the bird, the bark of the gun, the pheasant roasted in a tequila salsa that melts piquantly in your mouth.

I've served turkey at Good Samaritan hostels on Thanksgiving day, and I have ladled that white meat out and that great scoop of fluffed potatoes. But I was thinking that tame turkey has gotten so large in the breast (due to man's tampering), he can no longer mate. That wild turkey I shot for my own Thanksgiving dinner could mate. He was thin and rangy and chisel boned. He was wild and had the fire of God in him to reproduce his own kind. Not only did his breast stay out of his way, an oak tree wouldn't have been an interference.

JIM CULBERTSON

I was talking to Jim last night about this book, our hunts, our dogs. Jim made a great observation.

He said, "You know an English pointer seeks a big smell. Genetically and historically he's a covey finder.

"But the Lab, he has always been a fetcher. A one-bird fetcher. That's important to him—to find the bird. So he has become meticulous, thorough. He has always hunted hard for every 'single' bird and fetched it to hand."

Consequently, a shooting retriever searches hard to find every single bird, which means he is a single bird finder. All the difference in the world from the pointer. He is so much more thorough a hunter than the pointer.

The pointer glosses over; he hunts for miles; he's programmed for the big scent. You see it in the field trial write ups that say the pointer went out on a limb to find the bird. That means a single bird (or a covey) way off from all objectives, a fluke.

But the retriever has always worked close, never more than 40 yards for the most part. All his birds have been found on a limb, so to speak, never the main trunk of nature. The retriever always knew he had to find that one bird he was sent to fetch, so when he becomes a hunter, he becomes as thorough as an accountant. Which means that although the retriever has the greatest nose, he does hunt by sight when he closes. That's why the retriever is standing over those planted, tame birds and looking down at them. He wants to see them. He wants his eye to verify what his nose had indicated.

Everything Jim said makes glorious sense. Thanks, Pardner!

ENCASING THE PHEASANT IN CONCRETE

All Jim says above gives us a leg up in putting our retriever on preserve pheasants. But folks, those wild pheasants aren't going to hold like that. If you want a dog's point to paralyze that bird as though he'd received a lethal injection, then get a Wehle pointer.

I'll tell you what your VSR will do on these wild birds. As Jim says, "A Lab wants to fetch every single bird." This means that when a Lab with a big motor can work a pheasant sitting tight, he'll flat leap to fetch and knock the bird to sky for a sporting shot.

Or, as I've reported in other books, Keg of Black Powder, Jim's immortal bitch, once kicked a pheasant out of the rough at a municipal golf course (the links were closed for winter), and I shot the flyer from the first tee box. I've said before, "It was a hole in one."

Not only can a retriever flush wild birds, loop wild birds, block wild birds, and drive wild birds to your gun, but it can hunt laterally, and just by fool's luck, fly a gamebird right to your gun.

Mike Gould tells of blue grouse coming off a hill, sweeping down, making for a rim to drop off the Rockies at 10,000 feet, and Mike actually caught one in his hands. You'll recall Mike said he shot 60 percent of his game birds flying straight at him. I can tell you from years of duck hunting, it is a testy shot.

So, don't expect a hard point on a wild pheasant with a pointing retriever. It's done, I've had it done, I'll even enclose a picture here where it's being done. But the VSR is more likely to work the wild bird totally different than striving for a sight point.

THE COUSIN BOBWHITE

What you say for the snake tail, you can also say for the whistle bird, the bobwhite. The two birds would have the same habitat if there was enough lime in the soil for the pheasant. Anyway, that's a theory. But there's not enough lime, thus, no pheasant in Dixie.

Let's go to my favorite quest: the bobwhite. But first, let's teach you and Pup how to loop a pheasant field and drive the neon-bird to your gun.

Next chapter.

Putting Pup on Hand Signals or How to Hunt a Pheasant

Hand signal is not the term. It should be direction signals, because dogs will take a cast from any movement a man makes on foot, in a Jeep, or on a horse. The dog duplicates the movement he sees, what Mike Gould calls influence handling.

Web loops the field, so does Winston, and all Jim's dogs and mine. But these dogs have learned it naturally: they weren't taught. They are so bright they figured it out on their own because they recognized it was functional. They recognized what it did, and that was work!

But all dogs are not created equal. Some need training wheels and helmets, or at least they need you to run along to side and hold the bicycle seat. So let's do that.

Incidentally, everything we do in this chapter is going to get us a pheasant.

PUTTING PUP ON DIRECTION SIGNALS

There are many ways of doing this. Field trial aficionados could probably list 50. Me? I will list two: the baseball diamond drill and what Mike and Gary call influence handling.

THE BASEBALL DIAMOND

Pup doesn't know a baseball diamond from the Hope diamond, but he (she) does love to play games. Hurray! Here's one that becomes an obsession.

215

First, Pup must be rock solid on heel, sit, stay, and answer all whistle commands, especially the one abrupt blast that tells him to sit.

Walk him into the yard and heel him at home base. Now walk him to the pitcher's mound and seed the spot with big, stark-white dummies. Walk Pup back to home base, wheel him about, and cast him for one of the dummies. Repeat until all dummies have been gathered. Do the same thing at first, second, and third base.

Now sequester Pup and pile all your dummies on the pitcher's mound. Bring Pup to field and cast him for one dummy after another. Then retire Pup and do the same thing over and over for the three bases.

Okay, let's seed both the pitcher's mound and first base. This will guarantee that Pup is taking an exact cast off our hand. We send him to first base, to the pitcher's mound, and on and on.

THE BASE WITH NO DUMMY ON IT

Here's what we've been working up to: a destination with no dummy on it. There's nothing on the pitcher's mound–but there is on first base. Send Pup to the pitcher's mound and whistle for him to sit. He will turn to look at you and comply.

Now, don't just give a hand signal toward first base and tell Pup, "Over," or "Get over," or give a trill of the whistle, or whatever you're doing. Because handlers always do part of what the book says then innovate.

Extend your right arm and walk to the right–*the same direction as first base*–as you tell Pup, "Over." What you've just done is influence handling. Pup moves the way you move. I have found, because I've trained hundreds of dogs this way, you really don't need to say a thing, and that's the best. Too often in a pheasant patch, there's high-plains wind. The force just snatches your words and hurls them to South Dakota.

THE ENGLISH SPRINGER SPANIEL TRAINER

No one can teach direction signals better than a flusher trainer. That's the whole game. That's how he gets the dog to quarter–influence handling.

The way it's done is this: the man casts the dog left, but as the dog is leaving he throws a bird right. These guys have the unique ability to throw a bird the way you used to skip a pebble across a farm pond, and the bird sticks and stays planted. It's something to watch.

Anyway, the man whistles, Pup turns, and the man walks to his right. Pup does the same thing, which means he comes back toward the man, and further, that he is now running right. So what happens? He finds a bird. Wow!

And over and over and over, every time the flusher trainer whistles and the dog takes his body cast, the dog finds a bird. Don't you think that makes a believer out of that dog? The flusher trainer will tell you, "Never lie to that dog. Always finding a bird is the basis of the dog's success."

BACK TO BASEBALL

We've been playing ball with Pup for several days. We've progressed to the point where we have no dummies at the pitcher's mound, but they are seeded at every base.

We cast Pup to the pitcher's mound and toot him down. He looks at us, then he looks all about him. He wonders which dummy he'll be asked to fetch. You give him a back and he twirls about and runs to second base. Or you give him a direction to the left and he scoots to first. Do the opposite and he runs to third.

Or—and this is where it gets critical—you give Pup a cast to second base but when he's half way between second and the mound, you whistle for him to sit. Now you give him a cast to either first or second. This is when you learn if you have total control.

RETRIEVERS GET VERY SOPHISTICATED

So far we've sent Pup on 90-degree angles, right? Except for stopping him in front of second base and sending him to first. To do that he had to run a come-in oblique.

Well, retrievers are amazing. They can learn half signals. You can give angle backs or angle overs or, more to the point, suck-in adjustments.

I'll tell you what that's all about.

Say Pup's afield and you give him a back. He refuses for what-ever reason. Don't persist in making him disobey. Give him a suck-in whistle. Remember? One rolled tweet followed by a series of shorter tweets.

As you whistle, milk Pup in with your left arm, swinging it back and forth like a railroad brakeman. Also, to make all this more effective, walk to your left while your doing it, or walk at an angle which would be a left-back.

Pup will come to you. Remember place. Dogs know place. You get Pup moved off that place where he refused our direction signal.

Now you tell Pup back again, and he'll more than likely take it.

IT'S ALL VERY SIMPLE

It's all very simple, but sometimes there are problems, such as Pup can't run a straight line. So what to do now? Take him to the nearest school yard that has a chain link fence. Plant dummies at one end of the yard and take Pup to the other. Run him down the fence over and over, fetching those dummies. Put a straight line in him.

Also, go to center field of the school yard and plant your dum-mies along the fence, say 50 yards to the right of where you're standing. Now walk Pup 50 yards to field. Turn about and cast Pup straight toward the fence. Hit him with a whistle just as he is about to collide. Now give him an over (by walking that way), and he'll run a straight line down the fence (that 50 yards, remember?) to pick up the dummy.

Be prepared for lots of interference from bystanders. To them, this looks like magic, and they'll be asking you lots of questions. That's why it's best to visit the school yard when everyone's asleep or involved with something.

GARY RUPPEL

Gary starts direction signals (what he calls influence handling) when Pup is a baby. Pup will be called to him, and here he comes, waddling his fat tummy, just clearing the cover, his head high to drag a long stick.

Then Gary bends to the right at the trunk of his body. Honestly, the Pup will run that direction—the direction Gary is leaning. Try it. While this is going on, Gary is reading the pup. If

218

he sees the pup is losing interest, Gary will chatter (or tweet) and back up. This, too, is a direction signal. The Pup will speed up.

Should the pup stop, Gary stoops down and gets as low to the ground as he can. This automatically brings the pup to him because the man has taken a submissive role, which ends up being another direction signal.

If you ever have a dog afield that's frightened about anything or one that's about to bolt, be sure and go down to your knees to coax him to you.

GOING AGAINST THE GRAIN

Mike Gould is a proponent of going the wrong way with pups. That's how he gets total control on direction signals.

Here's how it works: if the Pup runs off, let's say, and he's going right, Mike doesn't say a word but begins walking left. He never looks back. He never signals the pup.

What Mike knows is that Pup does not want to break the bond, neither does he want to be ignored. And never alone, for now he finds himself far adrift in a strange field, and he wonders, "What's out there." So before long, he stops, turns, and here he comes.

That's the test: not to have the dog go the way you walk but to turn the dog from his own intent and have him follow you. Now you've got the dog on direction signals.

You'll realize that this is exactly what the flusher trainer is doing. The dog goes one way, the bird goes the other, the handler calls the dog to him and on past, and the dog finds a bird.

This is the interesting thing about shooting retriever pups. When Mike turns and walks the opposite direction (with his back to the pup), the pup never comes directly to him, to his side, or right before him—but instead, out to front. Out where he can continue hunting.

However, if Mike backs directly away and continually faces the pup, the pup will come to stand precisely before him or turn about to heel.

YOU DON'T HUNT PUP ON THE SALT FLATS

It's a rough world out there for Pup. There are hills, gullies, ditches, steep inclines. Pup's out there hunting but you want him to go another way. You realize then that there are several determinants on how well Pup does in obeying you.

First, does Pup have a dominant right or left paw? Consider, the dominant paw is always extended the farthest when Pup jumps a ditch, which means the recessive paw strikes dirt first.

Show and tell. Pup has a dominant right paw. He leaps and the left paw strikes dirt first. But that first leg always caves in a little bit upon striking, so Pup swerves (or is inclined to swerve) to the left. This means the right paw has to cross over for stability.

What's the consequence of all this? Pup comes out of that ditch off line. He's now canted to the left, so you have to hit him with the whistle, make him sit, then correct his line with a direction signal.

Why make Pup sit? Most hunting retrievers don't have the time to piddle with you—there are birds out there. If you try to give a direction signal with Pup standing, there's too great a likelihood he'll turn and leave you before you've even started your walk. Therefore, you make him sit to pay attention and to concentrate.

Now another thing. Do you know that most dogs will sour off a hill? That's right. Send Pup at a left oblique up a hill, and he'll drift off to the left—even more so. Knowing this, always cock Pup a little bit uphill, so that as he sours, he will come out exactly where you wanted him to go.

Hills are vital to Mike Gould because of the birds he likes to hunt. He wants those sky dwellers that fly down when busted up by a shooting retriever, like blue grouse and chukar. Whenever I ask Mike how 8-month-old Camas is doing, he always tells me, she's really running up the hill.

There are reasons for this. Chukar frequent the tops of those Flying B hills. Scarlet makes it up there and busts into a family of them, wow! A couple of successes like that and she will climb Mount Everest.

That's the point we've made all along. You can't train a bird dog without a bird. There has to be a reward for incentive. What value is a cotton-covered dummy or a tennis ball?

OKAY, ENOUGH OF THAT

What we're about here is getting Pup to loop birds far afield. Here's what we do now that he's on direction signals.

Duane Biggerstaff of Pueblo, Colorado, and Lab work stubble field to yield a cock pheasant. It was eight years ago when I hunted with this duo. My point is that many hunters have VSRs and have had for years. We just haven't paid attention.

221

We cast him far out at an oblique. By that, I mean you've read the cover and the terrain, and you have an idea where a cock pheasant might be. You cast Pup out and away from the bird.

Then you whistle for him to stop, give an "over" cast and send him to the objective. Here's the stopper: you usually hunt Pup into the wind, but now you realize he's looped back and is running with the wind and can't detect a scent cone.

Well, he'll be getting scent. There are foot tracks all over the ground, and his uncanny nose will tell him how old the scent is and which way the bird is going.

Pup will know when to be conscious and when to be bold, when to linger and when to attack. A seasoned dog will quarter toward you among the row crops. A pup will just run right in. But that's all part of it: growing up, learning, getting wise and competent.

There are so many things you should know about a dog. They don't like to run into the wind. were you aware of that? Oh, they'll cast straight out from your side into the wind. That's not the problem. But let them run across the wind, and you blow them down and cast them into the wind. No way, especially on water. It's just near flat impossible to get a retriever to take a cast into the wind when swimming.

Let's consider the dog looping. He's cast off into the wind: that's the way every hunt must start. But then he's asked to loop behind the birds and drive them to us. Well, a dog will roll with the wind more than he will against it. So here he comes. Yet, he's supposed to be hunting. A young pup will likely bust right through, and the next thing you know he's beside you. The old-timer will learn to quarter (as I said above) and take his time, even though the wind is now pushing him.

Another thing: cover.

DRIVING THROUGH A TANGLE

Some dogs are cover shy. It's hard to drive them through harsh vegetation: that is, to cast them away from you and hope they'll bust multi-flora rose or snow berry or Osage orange. But get the pup on the other side of the barrier and call him to you: he's coming. That's how you concentrate on getting Pup over cover shyness. Always bring him through the cover to you: never push him away to go through it.

222

Author's English setter and Lab display mixed bag. Setter has bobwhite and Lab has pheasant. Of course, the setter was taught to fetch, just as the Lab was taught to handle a scent cone.

If you have hills, you can put a good race into a pup by running him high. The wind currents are constantly ascending, and the pup is now running with the wind. What if there are birds on top? Well, Pup will over-run the birds, be on the upwind side, detect the scent cone, and loop back. Now he's going to chase and push the birds to your ground-level gun, and the fire that drives him is wild game scatting to avoid his lunge.

223

But, and this is interesting, any cover Pup runs into on his downhill quest is busted wide open. He's got momentum, he's got incentive, he's having fun.

A LOT OF GIVE AND TAKE

Heed this on direction signals. That's an invisible rubber band you've got attached to Pup's psyche. Not a taut rope about his neck. He'll respond in spurts or come fast part way, then slow. He's reasoning as he goes. He has other things on his mind beside you. So be patient, wait, watch, unravel his motives.

That's fun—to decipher what a dog's thinking or feel like you're doing that. Though I admit they interpret us far better than we'll ever interpret them.

Well, that's it for direction signals. With the material in this chapter, you can cast Pup to field, direct him sideways, whistle for him to drive the birds to you, and fire away.

However, there is a hazard here. Sometimes the cover is so high when hunting pheasants you can't see Pup a major part of the time. Keep whistling so he'll know exactly where you are and listen for disturbed cover. Pup will knock that stubble about.

The one thing we can't afford for Pup to do is exit sideways on a busy road. Should that be a possibility, then walking adjacent to that road is where you should be hunting or have a buddy monitoring out there.

Remember this: for a young pup to run up and jab his jaw out at an aged cock that's only wounded could result in the pup to getting a nasty gash across his nose. Pheasants have spurs, a killer instinct, and both speed and strength. If you see that bird kicking, don't let Pup jump it.

Tired of nothing to eat but pheasant? Then let's go for bobwhite.

※

Bobwhite

*This is gentry's bird, for those who can wear
hunting togs from Neiman Marcus. The pheasant
is a thug to them, so painted and squawky and
broad shouldered. But the jaunty quail sings in
the barnyard and can be seen sitting on tombstones
when you visit relatives, which means he's family.
Only Mickey Mouse, Bugs Bunny, and Smokey
the Bear have more admirers.*

Being born in Kansas and lingering long, I was granted the top
bobwhite hunting in the world. Before my era the classic bobwhite hunt was Dixie, but that's gone now.

Today's snowbird hunters throng into south Texas to have a go
at this bird on those baked greasewood flats, but the classic hunting of this bird is now the exclusionary property of southeast
Kansas.

AND WHAT'S CLASSIC HUNTING?

You hunt bobwhite much like you do pheasant except everything is more close in. That's because pheasant can be solitary-
while quail covey. The cover that quail prefer is tight, so the birds
are further bunched.

That one paragraph alone excludes Texas as a classic quail
venue. Where's the tight cover on those sprawling and arid
Mexican border ranches?

Kansas will confront you with great stands of dwarf pin oaks: a
tangle as formidable as old stockade walls. Then there's plum

thickets and stands of rank weeds (the quail love the seeds), and miles of soybean, milo, sudan and wheat stubble, and expanses of alfalfa, as well as the weed-clogged ditches. There are thousands of steep-banked and bush-clogged creek beds, and pond dams, stock tanks and flood control projects. A waterway in Kansas is a swale built with government money to stop erosion on a piece of land. Quail will be found up and down these waterways.

In other words, bobwhite are everywhere in Kansas. Not east of Wichita, mind you, though that can be proven wrong, too. But generally, southeast Kansas is the hunter's mecca, and you have access.

Try to get on a ranch in Texas where everything's owned and/or leased by insurance companies, banks, or some money interest. Hunts given as gifts to butter up their clientele with a day and a dog afield.

So what this means is simple: I know quail because I'm a Kansan, and there were years I did little else but chase their petite little behinds.

POINTS OF CONTACT

When you first meet a bobwhite, you usually encounter 8 to 20. Then you bust the covey and they scatter, which means you now hunt singles. For many hunters, because of their reflexes that ravel uninsulated when coveys explode, a single is the sure-fire way to go. Their non-insulated reflexes! I've had tyro hunters suffer a covey bust and go sit on a log, wiping their foreheads with a bandanna. It affects you like stepping on a snake. It's a hell of a nerve-wracking eruption.

The retrievers love it. They prompt a covey bust and leap after the exploding birds when you say, "Hunt em up," or whatever and they vacuum that place of the birds' departure. Their tails beating all vegetation flat, their noses separating the short grass, their hides gleaming, muscles shining, and when they look back to see where you are–they're smiling.

POINTS OF OPPORTUNITY

When you're around quail experts, you'll hear them talk about objectives or points of opportunity. What they mean by that is where you'll likely find this jaunty bird.

226

Jim and Wade Culbertson follow Labs down ditch in heavy cover. Bobwhite are nearby because we can hear their call.

We experienced much of this when we were teaching the VSR how to be steady to wing and shot. Remember? We'd mow a field but leave high clumps, or we'd gather and pile branches, which indicates that quail will congregate about an out-cropping. That's why they'll be at the foot of a windmill.

I've discovered bobwhite under a single persimmon tree, smack in the middle of 80 acres, where a pheasant might have been found loitering or traveling anywhere along the 80-acre way.

The big bird dogs that run on the classic field trial circuit will show you what I mean. They'll be coursing a pasture and make an abrupt right to descend a long slope and edge a small tank. Then they slam to point, and the handler flushes the birds.

These pointers know the birds seek prominent outcroppings, something distinctive. Remember the limb find. The big dogs don't bother much with that stuff. That lone persimmon tree would probably not get the average pointer's attention.

227

I told you bobwhite were close. Wade takes one to hand.

AS ALWAYS, THE EDGE

It's this simple. Kansas still has bobwhite because Kansas still has an edge. I was just out in the flower garden pulling weeds *from the edge*, and I realized edges are fertile. Hell, the weeds grow nowhere else.

Now agribusiness is trying to annhilate the edge, and will. But for the time being, they are still to be found.

228

Remember I said the bird was dead in Dixie? Primarily, this is because there's no more edge. I've had prime Tennessee bird cover removed by foreign interests to plant some row crop. Then they ripped out the hedgerow to get, say, 20 more rows of sunshine on the land.

When Dixie had the bird, Dixie had tenant farmers, sharecroppers, small operators. Six-acre units might have a patch of sorghum, a pea patch, some fruit trees, a barnyard with a cow and a mule, a horse to ride to town, some hogs in a dilapidated area. In other words, look at the pattern. Look at all the rows and fences and breaks in cover.

Now, take the Ames plantation where the national bird dog championship is run on quail. I forget, what is it–5,000 acres? Some 80 years ago, there were 250 tenant farmers on that land before acquisitions.

Everyone knows there are few birds on the Ames today. No edges is partially responsible. Others have big theories–even the ozone layer. Some say herbicides and insecticides. Could be. Sure would be likely candidates in my way of thinking. And the list goes on and on. But to what avail? As yet, no one has found a way to increase the quail in Dixie.

Also, quail don't eat cotton, or a lot of other pay-crops of today. Take John Bailey when he had the fabulous Quail Hills plantation outside Coffeeville, Mississippi. In off-season he would walk his 5,000 acres thumbing lespedeza seed out of his gnarled hand, then strike the seed into the soil with the heel of his boot.

John had lespedeza stands larger than federal buildings. John had cover and edge and feed. Get it? That's what quail demand. Take any one of these essentials away and you lose your birds.

THE SOIL BIRD

Above all else, bobwhite are dirt birds. Let me explain. They spend most of their day walking, scratching, dusting, and feeding on the ground. They're not in tree tops. They're on the ground. They seldom fly. They are always walking. They want clear, level freeways, and that's the bare earth requisite. Matter of fact, migratory birds fly; upland birds walk.

Quail prefer scattered short grass. I've had game preserve operators release birds in great stands of sedge in northern Mississippi. We never saw one of those birds the rest of the day. They probably suffocated in there. What a tangle.

Know this as well. Woodland suitable for quail is parklike. It's not a dense jungle. Birds wouldn't go there.

There is always the exception. You will find them in those tight pin oak stands in Kansas.

SUNUP

The birds awaken and feed an hour early in the morning. Then they gather in loafing country or what game biologists call woody-escape-cover for the rest of the day. What the hunter seeks and what the VSR must find when hunting bobwhite is food, roosting cover, loafing cover, nesting cover, escape cover, and brood cover, all based on bare ground.

Ground let's say that's never more than 50 percent in floral growth and never more than six inches high with foliage.

About 2 or 3 o'clock in the afternoon (what the Southerners call evening), the birds scatter out to feed again. They need a full crop when they go to roost. They will forage from one to two hours and then go to bed.

AND WATER

Experts argue bobwhite's dependency on water. Certainly, the bird can survive without drinking it, but you'll usually find a covey of birds favoring it. That's because of the oasis created where fresh buds continually appear and hordes of insects invade the area. Those insects contain moisture, and the birds eat them.

I've had game biologists explain that everything a bird does is related to two things: food and peril. He must eat, and he must keep out of sight (or range) of predators. That's his day: a day of survival. You and Pup are two of those predators the bobwhite must avoid.

HUNTING BOBWHITE WITH VSRS

What we'll do in hunting our VSR is run every edge and check ever feed source. Jim's dogs and mine course some 35 yards before us. A tweet will adjust them. Never a "sit" whistle but just a tweet. The dogs naturally stay grouped. Spread out no more than 8 yards from left to right, and some 3 yards from front to back. They move quickly, head down, thoroughly examining each piece of cover.

Then suddenly, the pack goes tense, the tails tremble and straighten, the shoulders pitch up and forward, a great scruff of hair may raise on the back of the neck. The dogs grow greatly animated, sweeping their heads faster, their tails beating more now. They move like halfbacks at a football game, twisting, contorting, leaning, swerving...searching for sight or scent.

Then up the birds come, and the dogs do one of two things: they either leap to fetch or stop and wait and turn to look at what we want them to do once the barrage has finished.

Some of the retrievers are continuing to hunt close, vacuuming the field, searching for every single bird. And look, a Lab leaps and bobs up with a bobwhite in his mouth, which he fetches to you live. Take the bird, send the dog on his way, and release the bird. Do that with the dog standing there, and you'll be called to canine court.

VSR Characteristics

The two prominent characteristics a VSR will display while hunting bobwhite are hesitation and scanning. Retrievers are so thorough they must check twice, thus the hesitation. They either move slowly when they think the goal is near, or quite quickly when nothing is sensed so they can make better time.

The nature of a retriever is to look at the least blade of grass. They are Sherlock Holmes in the bird patch. And know this: Retrievers on a hunt are amicable. No fighting ever. They dedicate themselves to helping each other. There's never jealousy or competition. They're all selflessly working for the same thing. Somehow they know a quail can hide beneath a blade of grass the size of a soda straw.

There is joy to a Lab finding a bird I've never seen in another living gun dog. Just look at one's face when he's fetching live: the way he tosses the bird to you and nuzzles your hand, touches your hand to show he loves you. He's serving you, he's yours, and you are his and the day is just the greatest.

The late Terry Smith of Savannah, Tenneessee, takes bobwhite from shooting retriever 10 years ago. Everywhere I hunted, I convinced others to put their Labs on bobwhite.

Remember, the pointer is out for the big smell but the Lab is intent (and content) in finding every single bird. Therefore, he'll hunt as long as it takes him to check every grass blade in an area. He'll never leave it if you tell him to stay. That's what we've inherited from a dog previously used as a retriever specialist. The retriever learned the value of every single bird.

THE PRESERVE BIRD

As always, the pen-raised bird does not provide the same sport as his wild cousin. I've had preserve birds perch on tree limbs and in order to shoot them I've had to throw clods to get them to fly. Why bother? I would prefer to throw grapefruit in the air and pop it.

232

This is one of Mike Gould's flight pens when he owned his own operation. Pheasant and chukar share this ensnared world.

To put the VSR in perspective, there's a story I've got to tell. It involves two gentlemen with professionally trained English pointers taking Jim and me quail hunting on a private corporate preserve. One of the gentlemen was the CEO (Chief Executive Officer); the other gentleman was his guest. As you can imagine, these gentlemen were our betters in so many ways. Like hunting with the Queen, you know?

En route to the operation, 100 banded quail were purchased, which means that when they were released, the party could harvest 100 tame or wild quail from the fields.

The CEO told Jim and me, "Shoot what you want."

Jim said, "You mean it?"

"If you can hit them," said the CEO, nudging his guest in the side.

I thought Jim's grip on his Model 12 barrel would bend it double. He managed to say, "Okay...there's a couple of run-down care homes that want our game."

"Fine," said the CEO, as he and his guest left with the two big pointers. Jim and I took off the other way with our pack of Labs foraging before us.

We met at lunch, where a bet was to be settled. We sat at a park bench with waiters dressed in white and black livery placing silver serving plates on white linen. I was given a salad not much larger than a poker chip. The CEO and his guest drank wine.   Yes, Jim and I were far out of our element.

Then the CEO asked, with a cocked eye toward his guest, "Well, how did you do…we got seven." Each of them smiled discreetly.

Jim and I looked incredulously at each other. Finally, Jim cleared his voice, adjusted his butt on the park bench, and in muffled voice, said, "We went by what the limit would be on wild birds. We got twenty."

"What?" asked the CEO.

Jim repeated the number.

There was to have been an afternoon hunt but Jim and I were not asked to stay.

What the heck? There was no way Jim and I could stop those Labs from busting that whole field of birds before us, and we only lifted to a sporting shot. It was a rout. All the birds Jim and I bagged were cleaned and taken to the folks at the care homes.

That should show the power of a VSR hunting bobwhite on a game preserve. If you want to make some money, just find a guy out there someday who favors his brace of pointers and scoffs at your black dogs rubbing about your legs.

I love to see black Labs vindicated.

✻

Hunting the Other Quail

Quail are notorious for running before a dog.
It's just that bobwhite stay cocked in the starting
blocks longer than the rest.

THE DESERT QUAIL

Favorite among the desert quail is the Mearns, the harlequin (clown, due to its graphic plumage) quail that dwells in the lower Sonoran desert some 5,000 feet aloft.

You'll find this national treasure among live oak trees, in tall grass stands, and in the shady side of hills.

I say national treasure because this bird is so beautiful and fragile and has the death-threatening need to favor principally one kind of food—the nut dug from under nut grass.

The government leases this dramatic bird's range to ranchers, and the cattle stamp out the nut grass and deny the Mearns a livelihood. I've seen Mearns habitat as bare as a pool table, with grass no higher than the felt.

Protesting to the national forest service, I've been told, "You don't understand. All the good land was taken up by ranchers. All the government got was the waste stuff private enterprise didn't want. Therefore, we don't have lush stuff to work with."

Ho, ho.

"That grass was like that when we inherited the land."

Ho, ho.

There's nothing we can do about it. The range cattle are going to kill out the Mearns, and that'll be one less game bird for the American sportsman.

Possibly the most beautiful of all quail, this Mearns was taken outside Patagonia, Arizona, in tall grass beneath a live oak.

CHARACTERISTICS

When it comes to running quail, Mearns linger just behind bob-white. The reason is that they live in very tall grass. Yes, a rare exception for a quail. Settled in deep grass they hope the dog will pass by and therefore, they become trapped and have to bust out in flight to escape. Consequently, they are available for a point and a flush. Also, they are the same size and weight and have the same flight-scat as the bob.

Opposite to chukar, this bird always flies uphill, then drops over the dome. He is nigh near impossible to find as a single. I quite frankly have never consistently found out where they go.

Their range offers prominently high cover for a quail: some 6 inches to knee-high of a man. But once again, the habitat is park-ike with great expanses between trees.

Since these birds make their living eating nut grass (albeit, a diet supplemented with berries, roots, and leaves) they require long claws to wrest this tough nut from the earth—claws so long and bent they cannot clutch a tree limb. The bird, therefore, spends his whole life on the ground.

Matter of fact, I've referred to their thin, arched nails being as awkward as those of a Chinese princess. Remember that gal in *Terry and the Pirates*, or are you too young for that?

THE POINT LAB

I've never owned a pointing Lab so I could not, therefore, hunt Mearns or any other bird with one. But I know these birds will hold for a pointer.

Remember, the birds are buried and that a Lab investigates each blade of grass. One day a covey is going to look up at a curious black face, and that will be the first Lab point on a Mearns quail.

The retriever will hold the bird, because their home is so grass-deep the birds will not be able to loft and fly. They've had it, and they'll know it.

THE FLUSHING LAB

When I first moved to Arizona (prior to migrating on up to Nevada), I brought a Labrador derby champ from my large Kansas kennel operation named Super Scooper of Vondalia. Scoop was a flusher, no ifs, ands, or buts. He'd hit that cover and knock those birds skyward, and there was no way to hold him back from doing it.

Scoop was that way—self-determined. I've mentioned him in other books. You'll remember he could never become a field trial champion because he refused to sit anywhere his testicles would get wet.

Well, anyway, Scoop proved for all of us a flushing Lab will bring Mearns to the gun. Not with a point, granted, nor a delayed whoa, but a leap so mighty you'd think Scoop was playing Australian football.

Here's the way it goes. A Lab has a nose superior to practically any other canine. Scoop would wind the bird. He'd barge on, though, not tip-toeing into the scent cone, his head ever swinging like radar, his nose low, his ears high, his tail beating fast, and his pelvic drive muscles clumped for a leap.

Then, when he had everything zeroed in, he'd fly in a great arc and come down with the configuration of a praying mantis and birds would explode. Not that second because it took them a time to make their way to the top of that hindering clumped grass. But then they would explode, and Scoop would usually have a live bird in his mouth.

This delayed-flush gave me a chance to mount my aluminum Franchi, and I'd be on the birds when they cleared. You can do the same.

THE RECLUSE BIRD

A trait of the Mearns I admire is that he's like me. He shuns any type of improvement, any type of human habitation. He wants to live on top of the mountain, far, far away, with an unlisted number.

In that regard, he's also like the Siberian Ibex I hunted in Mongolia. There is minimal vegetation there, primarily outcrop rocks. Therefore, should a hunter peer around a corner, the herd of Ibex will see the hat brim in a flash and explode to flight.

The Mearns listens. That's the comparison I would make to the Ibex. They look, they listen and know the second you invade their territory, and hunker down in that tall grass, which is to their peril if you have a full-bored Lab that can snatch scent 80 yards away.

Plus, by nature, a Lab is going to sniff out every recess. The birds are doomed.

HOLSTER THE GUN

When hunting for this unique bird, please don't consider taking the Arizona limit. Take one at most and have it mounted, or take two for dinner.

These Gamble's quail can be found in most any suburban or rural yard. They are a delightful bird, a joy to accompany, a test to hunt, and a treat to serve at suppertime.

But holster your gun, please. This bird has minimal foraging range and is reluctant to leave it. The government doesn't care if he's rendered extinct, since they will do nothing to get the cattle hooves off his roof.

And in that regard, roof is not a misnomer. The female places her eggs in a hole and weaves a thatch roof to flap over it. Unique!

So hunt the bird, but don't shoot it. Okay?

And in that high country of southern Arizona, enjoy some of the most beautiful vistas in the world. And the weather? Wear shirt sleeves in January. As for eating something other than Mearns, don't pass by a Tex-Mex cafe. There's good eatin' in there.

GAMBLE'S QUAIL

When I lived on a mountain side in Phoenix, Arizona, and later at some 4,000 feet in rural Sedona, the Gamble's quail joined me at both places—in my yard, in my juniper trees, in my drive. Everywhere. And he was adored and welcome. Often he'd fly by as I was char-broiling a steak or hamburger, perch in the ever-green trees and make a murmur like a glunk. Another aspect of his character that intrigued me is his love of babies. He'll flat steal a hatch if he can and prove to be a dutiful mother.

OL' SCOOP

Scoop loved to chase these birds, sometimes to reward. We'd go out in the desert and kick about for them, knowing we could encounter this jaunty bird with the black topknot anywhere from 1,000 to 4,000 feet.

Albeit, the lower-elevation population favored a riparian set-ting, and the high altitude dwellers could be found during hunting season in great sweeps of dried and brittle grass, on land rolling and pinching into dry arrows and festooned with rocks left by an exploding volcano.

Scoop and I undertook these hunts knowing we were in for a rough time of it, since the birds run like gazelles and make a testy target when aloft. Sort of dipsy-doodle like a woodcock.

HUNTING

The important thing to remember about hunting Gamble's is they are hard to find, difficult to be near for a covey rise, and if shot at, will seldom be seen again.

Scoop proved a natural handler since he hit them so hard they thoughtlessly scrambled 360 degrees (instead of going straight away), and I always got off two shots. It was easy for Scoop to ambush Gamble's since they stayed in open country and their scent carried far distances.

RECONNOITERING GAMBLE'S QUAIL

Now, on your first encounter you may get some birds because Gamble's have this unique trait: if they are ambushed, they have a staging area, a place to go, a haven. Predesignated, preplanned. Should you find that haven, the bird is without wit to find another place to hide. A grass-parting Lab will uproot almost every single bird hunkering in that haven.

However, once the Gamble's has gone through a covey rise and then an ambush at the staging area, you'll likely never find this bird again. They hide forever. They're like that old adage: *Make a fool of me once and that's your fault. Make a fool of me twice and the fault is mine.*

The Bird

When winter snows are starting to melt in the highlands, Gambles feed on the leaves and flowers of mimosa, palo verde, and mesquite. Seeds from locoweed, lupine, and deer vetch also constitute a good part of their intake.

As the nesting season develops, the birds switch some to insects and ants.

During the hunting season you should concentrate your quest on brush areas sporting thorny legumes. Shrubbery and cacti also announce an early winter locale for these birds. If sufficient shrubbery is present in grasslands, you'll find the birds loafing there.

Also, look for winter sport along saltbush-clogged creek beds, featuring arrow-bean and salt cedar. Check all irrigation channels and shrubbery-ladened fence rows. As always, clean farming and overgrazing constitute the bird's worst enemy. Traditionally dry or partially dry, river beds with brush-tangled banks and fresh greens inland have made up the best hunting sites for this bird.

At high elevations you'll find Gambles in piñon and juniper stands, or even in pines. You just might say Gamble's are where you find them. All in all, they prefer to feed on the production of winter annuals. They are the most widely scattered game bird in Arizona and surely the easiest to find.

Scaled Quail

To hunt a scaled quail must be a lot like hunting mustangs in the old days. You've got a race on your hands, or more precisely, your feet.

These birds scat. A silver bird with a white "cotton-top" and a scaled breast that resembles the back of a carp, this dry-land dude can seemingly survive on hot air.

The scaled quail will give you and your dog a merry chase. If you don't have time and legs, then go shoot pool.

What's out there in his habitat to eat? And where's the cover to say nothing of the edge.

You've got great expanses of nothing, of greasewood or alkali flats, of bed rock, or duned sand, and leafless trees, and scrub cactus.

Web Parton, my dog training and hunting buddy out of Oracle, Arizona, talks and writes of "sky islands," where he harvests these quail. But know something inherent in this statement.: Parton has that ability to climb 90-degree walls, and he does it carrying 8 quarts of water for his dogs. After all, he is in the desert, and he does pamper his charges.

Web probably harvests more game birds in Arizona than any other hunter. Where I see barrenness in the scaled quail's domain, he sees a variety of vegetation, even describing some of it as lush.

WHAT'S REALLY OUT THERE

Scaled quail reside in the Chihuahuan desert, semidesert grassland, and the dwindling fringe of plains grassland. You'll come upon them in Texas, New Mexico, and Arizona. Remnant populations are reported in Colorado, Kansas, Oklahoma, and surprisingly, in irrigated country of northern Nevada and in the state of Washington.

All scaled quail prefer wide vistas made up of grass expanses. Opposite to the Gambles, they shun thick tangles. Their favorite foods include soapweed yucca (that Indian ladies prefer for shampoo), acacias, mesquites, Russian thistle, pigweed, sorghum, acacia, and prickly pear fruit in season.

This bird favors warm temperatures and is usually not found anywhere that the annual precipitation exceeds 6 inches. However, as it always is with nature, some scaled quail can be found in rainy mountains as high as 7,000 feet. But if I were you, I'd not spend my time looking there. This is not what Web means by "sky islands."

He means, come fall the scaled quail will usually leave the arroyo-cleaved flats and climb the foothills, favoring rougher terrain than they sought below. There, and above, are the "sky islands."

HOW TO HUNT

You generally hunt scaled quail by pushing them to an edge, say an arroyo, a brush-edge ditch, an irrigation channel, or stock tank, anywhere there might be thick vegetation for the bird to hide.

Having run there and seeing you persist in following him, the bird hesitates to break out and try his luck going away on the other side. So he waits for the dog. He doesn't know that, but he does.

And here comes the dust-clogged Lab. It's hot, he's dry, and thirsty and his eyes are red from dust. Nevertheless, he sniffs about and more slowly than with a cool-weather bird, he attacks the hide. Generally, the scaled quail will fly. Unique to his species, he'll attempt a space probe coming out of there, straight up, nearly. And you wait for him to apex before shooting.

Because of this and the fact scalies can jump before you get near them, you'd better carry a heavy, long-range gun even though you're in walk-a-marathon country with a high temperature.

You shoot, gather your bird(s), wipe your brow, look off at those dust devils, or those neon-snakes writhing from the heated flats, and decide whether you want to continue this hunt. However, there is this: next to the Gamble's quail, the scaled quail is the most heavily populated bird in this arid country. There is this other thing. The scaled quail is possibly the easiest of all quail to hunt as singles.

You can see forever out there and designate where the covey lands. You walk to the locale, cast your dog for close work, keeping on the tweet whistle, and as the birds come up–often far away–you reach out with your 30" barrel, 12-gauge auto.

But when a scaled quail covey lands, there's the likelihood the birds will run. So send your VSR way out and about in hopes he can turn some birds back to you–birds that have hunkered down on the flat and will only move to the dog's encroachment.

Don't ever enter the desert without water. You need it, your dog needs it. Be equipped.

California Quail

Also called valley quail, this pert bird gives Westerners a lot of sport and can be easily hunted with a VSR, especially when a hunter encounters a covey of them numbering into the hundreds. Yes, this is one bird that does flock together.

You'll find California quail around irrigation projects, parklike woodlands, bush-clogged creek bottoms, cultivated land, vineyards, and let's say–nearly everywhere.

A requirement of this bird is to roost in tall, dense foliage. He just wants privacy. The birds can be traced by seeking out their favorite foods, which are many. These include gooseberry sage, snowberry, elder, manzanita, bur clover, lupin, ocotillo, mimosa, fillare, mesquite beans and alfalfa.

There's no finer eating bird, since this guy's diet is over 95 percent vegetable.

Hunting Characteristics

I said above that this is a sporting bird for many reasons. Like the scaled quail, this bird gives you an exploding rise, not a measured exit like a Gamble's that seems programmed for low-altitude bombing.

244

Nor does the bird just set its wing and glide. He's got evasion tactics built into his flight plan. Then, when he hits he runs, but if you close, or your dog closes too fast, the rascal will loft again.

I don't know how a pointing Lab could handle a covey of these fidgety birds. You can't crowd their covey, and the Lab wants to sight point, so that's out.

I get into them by just having the retriever roar forward and knock them up. Pell mell, as it were.

But the most productive scheme is to have a looping retriever cast about and sandwich the birds between himself and your gun.

Once again, you're shooting a far-away bird and need heavy artillery to reach them

Like chukar, the California quail does not always afford an easy hunt. You've got upright walls, sheer drop-offs, limb-woven creek bottoms, high grasslands, and irrigated fields. You're going to be looking and walking a long, long way.

Mountain Quail

On this bird I'd just say forget it. To start with, the bird lives on vertical mountain sides in cover that defies entry. Okay? You want more?

Hunters have occasionally taken off after these birds and never harvested more than three in a lifetime. They run, they're in dense thicket, and you can't see them. The stuff is so impenetrable, a dog can't get through it. So how are you going to flush them? Mountain quail seldom fly.

If you demand a hunt, however, then here's what you do. Climb the mountain to gain the highest ridge. Hunting season comes during high heat, so sit awhile and see if you're going to die.

Now stand and start back down, dog at heel–that's right. If the dog goes in front he'll flush the birds out of range for sure. This is a spooky bird.

The occasional flight features a leaping take-off and then a maneuvering, for this bird knows how to put obstacles between himself and birdshot.

I repeat, you're going to confront this bird in a brush tangle, say manzanita, which is impenetrable and the only way you can access it is on your knees and your Lab is scooting on his belly.

Let's say the birds are going to jump. How the hell are you going to stand up and shoot? You're not.

So why are you out here hunting this hunt-proof bird? Because he's the largest quail in the nation (he's a foot long), maybe the prettiest, what with that drum major's plum, and he is a true wilderness character.

You can't point a mountain quail–the birds are gone before you know they were there. So a Lab's role is usually to just fetch what you shoot, although a looping Lab might push these birds to you if he could maneuver the matted cover.

CONCLUSION

Quail are not necessarily the premier game bird in America, but they've always been where I've lived so I've gotten to know them. Just like Ben Williams knows those Hungarian partridge–they're in his backyard.

There are other birds as testy, as hard to hit, as hard to find. They range from the predictability of the bobwhite to the ambush-proof mountain quail.

They all come to the table well, and there's never a closed season. However, that's not going to last forever with Mearns.

Most quail love habitation and are seen daily by passersby. They become a friendly fixture of rural or suburban life.

I hunt many species of bird, but I have a fondness for quail. They stir the psyche, fit the hand, tantalize the dog, and are usually found in postcard country.

Now for the Hungarian partridge, sharptails, and prairie chicken.

※

Hungarian Partridge, Sharptails, and Prairie Chicken

There are three game birds that await you on a high hill. Here's how to bring them down to your level.

Ben Williams and Winston have taught us how to hunt Hungarian partridge and taught us well. You'll see below why their looping tactics win the day.

When a Hun knows he's being stalked, he takes off running in a swivel-hipped course. If he's forced to fly, however, he has a covey bust more dynamic than a bobwhite, so he is a prized trophy.

Having lifted, the Hun is a long-flight bird, sometimes traveling a half-mile. You'll remember Winston chasing them.

A Hun's primary defense is to attain the most prominent hilltop and loaf there, eyeing for intrusion. That's why Williams and Winston traverse the hills instead of walking the gullies between them—they're cross-winding those high roosts.

There's no use following a busted covey for the singles. Once the bird lands he'll usually run another 200 yards. So Winston loops the birds and drives them to the gun. The birds want to run, anyway. Let them run to the hunter. Should they flush, then that's the best of all shots—coming right at you.

SHARPTAIL GROUSE

This bird occupies the same venue as the Hun. They live wing-tip to wing-tip. However, unlike the Hun that prefers more or less open country, the sharptail enjoys brushy and woody cover.

Sharptail also mount the hilltops to monitor their surroundings. They, too, have an exciting loft from flush, but unlike the Hun, bore straight away instead of giving you that feint and go.

The sharptail means the death of the bobwhite. Strange? Not really. All the big time pointer pros head for the Dakotas and Canadian prairies for summer training. The pups learn on sharptails (which don't fly well in summer's heat), then they are switched to bobwhite upon returning to their home kennels in Dixie.

All this is brought about by old buffalo wallows, great indentations in the prairie floor, called bluffs. The sharptail fly from one of these mini-habitats to the other. The trainer, then, can cast his pointers to a wallow, get a point, watch the lazy flight to the next bluff or to some grass clumps in between, and repeat the training.

Over the years water has pooled in these buffalo depressions and sprouted what's called wolf willows. Actually the copses are aspen and poplar.

Anyway, why are the dogs easily driven to these trees? Because in summer's inferno the sharptail "noon" in there, beating the heat. The bluffs are literally loaded with birds. There's something else. When a flight of sharptails land, they scatter out and offer maximum single work.

What all this means to you is this: if sharptail season opens on a hot day, you're going to get your VSR into maximum dog work, either pointing, whoaing, flushing, or yes, even looping.

But on a cool day? Forget it. Now you've got a wary bird with his hand on the stick shift, and he's ready to peel rubber. Now you must loop and drive.

PRAIRIE CHICKEN

In the old days Jim Culbertson and I would take a stand in the darkness along a fence row and hope to sit there and intercept the flight of prairie chicken as they made their way to a soybean field. But that got ornery, since any bird dropped would be claimed by everyone on the row.

So Jim and I took off to the flinthills, a limitless prairie of repeating domed hills, where we would walk up and down, over and over. The only trees there grow in the deep swales at the bottom of the more prominent domes.

Once again, the prairie chicken, like the sharptail and the Hun, seeks high promontories to check all approaches. Consequently, to hunt him like you do quail, you've got to climb many a hill for many a mile.

We've had Labs walk right up to a covey of chicken and take one more step and the birds erupt. It was a delayed whoa, if you will. You'll recognize this about shooting retrievers. They self-adjust for each species of game. They approach chicken in an entirely different way than they do bobwhite, for example.

A case in point is the Labs would loop pheasant on a Saturday hunt, but the next day, and 125 miles east, they would stalk prairie chicken face-on. I never had a Lab naturally loop about and try to drive a prairie chicken to me. That would have worked because a chicken is a downward flying bird, like a chukar or a blue grouse.

I guess the problem was that those hills are so slightly inclined and so massive–being a mile wide sometimes–I'd have had to cast the dog a mile around to come back for the high bird.

But with shooting retrievers you can hunt this bird like long-distance quail and eat chicken that night.

Now let's cast for chukar and blue grouse.

This hunter borrows a part of Mike Gould's training pack and successfully hunts blue grouse.

Chukar and Blue Grouse

*Here are two birds best looped and driven
from a high rim from whence they'll drop
off and glide to your waiting gun below.*

These are Mike Gould's birds: the resident master. They play
the game he loves. He casts Web to a stand of aspen for blue
grouse, the birds erupt and fly toward the rim of the park (in the
Rockies, any clearing in the woods), and Mike waits there to pot
them coming head-on.

Or, and this must have been picturesque, on Idaho's Snake
River Mike floated in a canoe, listened for the chukar's "chuck,"
and cast Web high around and past the outcrop rim. Then miracle
dog Web drove the chukars off their loft, and they would dive to
meet Mike's waiting gun.

CHUKAR

Nancy Sinatra had a hit song in the '60s titled, "These boots are
made for walking." Chukar are, too.

Their natural habitat is lonely vistas, great expanses of high
chaparral, wind blown haunts, rimrock, gritty land that is sharp-
edged, sand blasted, and deeply eroded.

They prefer hot weather. One hundred degrees is not abnor-
mal. So there you are, climbing mountain sides, slipping and sliding on loose-based gravel and sand, lugging canteens of water,
and toting a heavy gun, because if the birds do get up, you've got
a far-away shot. (Note: all chukar experts recommend you carry a

light gun because they are forever climbing, trying to get a dog over the birds. The consensus is a .20 gauge.)

THE LOOPING VSR

You can also take a looping VSR and avoid all this strain and discomfort. Chukar are infamous for running uphill, flushing into the wind, and gliding back down. All you need, then, is a dog that drives them up so they will exit, and a looping VSR will do it.

A characteristic of this bird is that a couple of chukar are usually left behind. These are the call-back birds, and if you were up there, you could have Pup flush them and put them in your bag. But we aren't up there, and we aren't going to be up there, so they can call to their heart's content.

Should Pup climb the mountain side and burst right out on the chukar, they'll panic and flush whichever way the wind is blowing, and glide. However, if you can cast Pup up an adjoining incline, get him on top, then loop him out and about the birds, they will know he's coming and jump off with less panic and probably glide right to your gun.

That's not to say that while Pup is climbing, he won't kick chukar out of brush; he will.

SANDWICHING

When the chukar alight in the lowlands, they turn right around and walk back up the incline. So if Pup's whistled in, and he's descending, once again he'll meet and loft the birds back to your stand.

WATER

Another way to hunt chukar is to jump their water holes. Due to the heat and the activity of the bird, these guys seek water several times a day. You'll find tanks or ponds or depressions filled with water that are completely imprinted with chukar track.

Chukar are a tough bird to bag. It's a physical hunt and both dog and hunter better be in good shape. A chukar hunt can become as serious as a heart attack.

The blue grouse is a handsome, hefty bird that makes a delightful hunt and a great meal.

BLUE GROUSE

We know a few things about blue grouse since we've been talking about, or talking to, Mike Gould and this is his specialty bird, as mine is bobwhite.

You'll recall blue grouse love to congregate in male aspen stands. Now you're talking altitude: say 7,000 feet and up. The birds can be found at lower elevations during particular months of the year, but high-up is where you'll encounter them during nesting and hunting season.

Like the chukar, this bird's favorite escape maneuver is to loft, turn, and glide down. Consequently, you can send a VSR to loop about and drive them to you. They'll stay relatively close to the ground as they beat toward the rim and can even pass a man, head-high.

If you spend a morning hunting aspen and don't meet a blue grouse, then switch to seepy springs, stands of fescue, or rimrocks.

253

You'll remember that when we started our bird hunting in this text, I told you we needed a VSR with thrust and independence. At no time is this more applicable than when hunting blue grouse. The dog can work at such far distances he must be totally in charge, know exactly what to do, and do it as he wants.

He has no help; he is alone, distant, and trustworthy. This is a VSR at his finest. No wonder Mike so loves this bird.

THE SUNSHINE BIRD

When hunting this bird, don't overlook areas of saturated sunshine. Blue grouse crave it. I've often seen them standing on a rimrock, say 3,000 feet above landfall (10,000 feet above sea level), with the early sun warming their mottled plumage.

That sun, incidentally, also brings to life much of the feed these birds seek, so their sunbathing has a dual purpose. They can also snack.

Maybe when it's all said and done, the reason I like to hunt blue grouse is as much the scenery and the clean air as it is the bird. It's invigorating to hunt at tree line. Sauntering under a brilliant and clear sun, looking off at multiple snow-capped mountain ranges, stepping across murmuring and clear-flowing rivulets, snapping a branch for the heady scent of pine. Yes, Rocky Mountain high and blue grouse are a great combination.

And taking this bird to the char-broiler is one of my favorite things.

❊

Sage Grouse, Ruffed Grouse, and Woodcock

This chapter highlights our largest upland game bird, the most revered, and the strangest. Not that the odd woodcock is upland game, but he has a natural meld of upland and shorebird characteristics and is a Godsend for the gun dog trainer.

When you're talking sage grouse you're talking Big Bird. It's as though he ought to jump off the screen of Sesame Street. But you're not talking about some dust-country dodo. Far from it. This bird is bright, highly tactical, and faster than a bobwhite, or else he'd be extinct.

To cut out cross country with your pack and expect to harvest this bird poses a great challenge, but then you turn around and do something no more dramatic than come around a bend in your car and there the sage stands in the middle of a dirt road. You let the dogs out, leave the road to be legal, walk a long way around to stand somewhere afield next to the bird, then tell the VSRs to knock the bird to sky.

NATURE

This bird eats little else but sage grass. Hence his name. The sage grouse is unique among birds, since he has no muscular gizzard. Consequently his thin-walled stomach requires soft foods, and that's the soothing nutrition of sagebrush.

Mike takes stand in immense landscape of Colorado at 10,000 feet. Web will soon knock the blue grouse to sky, and they'll come diving past Mike's stand as they rocket downward.

Sage brush can impart a rank taste to this bird's flesh and that plagues many outdoor cooks bringing an edible bird to the table.

We're talking about a 6½ pound bird here, nearly two feet long. Learn to cook him and you've got a pot of food that will outlast a blizzard.

HUNTING

When seeking sage grouse, stick to arid and semiarid country and never hunt a region where snow can cover the bird's required sagebrush. No bird will be there, ever.

Any sage grouse hunt can entail miles of walking over endless, empty expanses of land, both windblown and forlorn.

If all else fails and your feet give out on an arid hunt, then sit by any water hole where you can detect sage grouse tracks. These birds do come to water. Keep concealed and you might get lunch. But such a stand-still hunt offers little sport for the VSR.

256

Author holds blue grouse that the Lab at right drove to him.

After sitting by the pond until you're rested, cast Pup before you and walk in ever widening circles about the water hole. The birds come to drink several times a day and you might encounter them coming in.

RUFFED GROUSE

This is the imperial bird of eastern gentry. Ancient coastal etiquette requires this bird be hunted by long feathered black and white Llewellyn setters backed up by tweed-clad shooters sporting Holland and Holland or Purdy side-by-sides.

To imagine a retriever beating about the bush would cause a monocle to drop and the brace of a third brandy at the Sheeps Head Inn. That's because these sportsmen don't know the VSR can get you into birds.

257

And yes, it does take a particular VSR to get that job done due to the fact this bird is more spooky than a cat burglar. But there is a type of retriever that can pull it off.

That retriever would be the Chesapeake, Maggie. Remember Butch Goodwin's Maggie? Maggie is slow, patient, silent, and solid. She would edge her way up to the bird and stand there, pointing. That doesn't mean the ruffed grouse would be there by the time beefy Butch brawled his way through the tangle, but the bird would have spooked from his approach, not Maggie's.

Coming from Kansas, ruffed grouse was never a life goal of mine. I'd have to leave the state to encounter the guy. Each time I'd hunt back east or up toward Canada I'd vow to return in the summer with a chain saw and cut some grouse corridors. How do those Easterners get through that tangle?

Then there's the other thing. Practically every time I hunt grouse it rains, and what bird are you going to find beating about in the drizzles?

So you're walking in that morass of cross limbs—in a downpour—and it's not only peppering through the foliage but it's dripping off each limb and I'm going to turn to my Lab and say, "Pardner, ain't we having a swell time."

Of course he won't care. When would a water dog object to rain?

A WOOD BIRD

Grouse are dense-wood birds. You'll find them in aspens, apple trees, willows, catkins, hazelnut, and wild cherry. Any place that is seemingly dark and impenetrable will attract him. That's why you should kick every wood pile, briar patch, weed wall, grass tangle, and Jeep-proof thicket.

During deep winter the hunter should also check the snowbanks, because ruffed grouse have the knack of diving straight into them and, like a sled dog, taking a warm snooze.

Traditionally, no dog can possibly hunt this bird that doesn't stop at the absolute outer edge of the scent cone. Encroach on that cone and you've lost your bird. I mean this is the most jumpy bird on earth. They should wear a shoulder patch declaring: Evacuation At All Costs!

So what chance does a VSR have? Well some. Always remember the slow-paced Maggie. A rip-snorting, hi-flying, limb-cracking VSR is not going to get you a ruffed grouse. Unless! Unless he loops about and startles the bird to you.

But that's whistling in New England, for how is the hunter ever to see through those limbs, woven as tight and compact as steel wool, and locate a sitting grouse? So a loop that would produce a grouse would be about as likely as winning the lottery.

Another reason a VSR may not be considered a good ruffed grouse dog is that all grouse dogs are expected to hunt close to the hunter, and that's not our VSR. Our VSR has thrust and independence, remember? We've been looping him about chukar 300 feet up an incline. Now we want our knees to bump him as he walks.

But I'm going to tell you something about those hunters who want a dog to hunt close: they've never had a trained dog. It's that simple.

But it has happened. Yes it has. VSRs have already brought ruffed grouse to bag. As the pointing retriever gene pool develops and we can field long-range pointing retrievers, we'll be delivering more grouse to hand.

WOODCOCK

Remember my needling Mike Gould about hunting woodcock since they were not found on an incline, and he hum-hawed around? Why not? Woodcock haven't been a plentiful bird for him. And, anyway, I was pulling his leg.

He is so thoroughly given over to incline hunting, where the retriever loops the bird and pushes it down, then as the dog descends to the canyon bottom, he meets the flushed birds waling back up. And flushes them again!

Well anyway, woodcock is not an upland bird. It just looks like one.

Woodcock are worm-eating, mud dwellers, with spiked beaks, eyes in the back of their head, and a body as round as a hand grenade.

They'll hold for a dog's point. That's the beauty of them. But they'll spook with explosive speed if the hunter appears. You've

Here's Pecos, the author's current shooting Lab, hunting.

got to shoot fast and throw enough shot to knock this erratic-flying bird to earth.

Not only does hunting season provide great sport with this bird, but he makes a fabulous training bird on his northern migration come late winter. February training sessions on passing woodcock are becoming an institution in several northeastern states.

Where I meet woodcock is hunting bobwhite along boggy creek banks. They'll flush with the quail, and you'll know it. They fly with all the zest of a released balloon.

Also, the woodcock feeds at night so the dog will point him in bed the following day. Consequently, the bird will be holed up in roosting cover, quite well concealed and camouflaged.

Should you be lucky enough to hit one of these guys don't be surprised if your retriever refuses to fetch him up. Woodcook have a horrible odor to a dog.

May all your days afield be good days, and all your dogs be good dogs.

IN CLOSING

So that's it. We've trained our VSR and now we've put him on all likely upland game. You'll recognize his great strength lies in hunting bobwhite and blue grouse. His poorest performance will come on ruffed grouse and mountain quail. These birds are so elusive they could escape radar.

I've had a lot of fun joining you in this journey through shooting retrieverdom. It's a new and fascinating sport, one that will grow in leaps and bounds once hunters find the production that can come from a pack of retrievers seeking upland game.

Don't ever forget the story about the CEO, his guest, and their seven birds. That story tells it all about the value of a shooting retriever.

But that's not the whole of it and never will be. Retrievers are mellow. They're soft and caring and sympathetic. They love man and live to do him good.

You're out there hunting now and thinking, that dog up there is the best I ever had.

One day, when all this is past, you may realize that dog was the best friend you ever had.

Be kind.

Trainer Information

Jim Charlton
The Charlton Kennels and Farm
13825 NW Charlton Road
Sauvie Island, OR 97231
503-621-3675

Butch Goodwin
Northern Flight Performance Retrievers
4965 Freemont Road
New Plymouth, ID 83655
208-278-5367

Mike Gould
1116 South Peach
P.O. Box 161
Kamiah, ID 83536
208-935-2663

Gary Ruppel
Gun Dog Specialist
8823 Prickly Pear Creek
Parker, CO 80134
303-699-9660

Index